3-6
75

THE CHASE. *Misericords from* 1. *Ely Cathedral (14th cent.);* 2. *Boston, Lincs (late 14th cent.);* 3. *Beverley Minster (early 16th cent.)*

CHAUCER

The Nun's Priest's Tale

EDITED BY

KENNETH SISAM

OXFORD
AT THE CLARENDON PRESS
M DCCCC XXVII

Oxford University Press

London   Edinburgh   Glasgow   Copenhagen
New York Toronto Melbourne Cape Town
Bombay   Calcutta   Madras   Shanghai
Humphrey Milford Publisher to the UNIVERSITY

Printed in England at the OXFORD UNIVERSITY PRESS
By John Johnson Printer to the University

PREFACE

IN preparing this edition I have had in mind the needs of schools and colleges who keep up the good practice of studying a few short texts minutely, and of including *The Nun's Priest's Tale* among them. As not many users of the edition will come to it with a grounding in medieval literature, or with an adequate library at hand, it seemed best to give a minimum of references to books and articles, and to include a good deal of elementary matter which those who do not need it may pass over.

The notes of Tyrwhitt, Skeat, and Mr. Pollard (in his separate edition) have eased the way for commentators on this tale; and Mr. Griffith's *Bibliography of Chaucer 1908–1924* (Washington 1926) has been my guide to some recent articles. Mere difficulty of access has prevented me from using Miss Petersen's thorough study of the sources as much as I could have wished, but I have gone over again points of difference in the results.

For help in obtaining the illustrations from carvings, I am obliged to the authorities at Beverley Minster, Boston (Lincs.), Carlisle, and Ely, and to the photographers, the Rev. W. E. Wigfall, and Messrs. G. E. Hackford, F. W. Tassall, and G. H. Tyndall. Canon Christopher Wordsworth very kindly gave me an account of the early fox carvings in the Chapter House at Salisbury, but they were much broken before restoration, and they throw no light on our story.

K. S.

CONTENTS

ILLUSTRATIONS

INTRODUCTION

I. THE BEAST FABLE.

STORIES of animals are found in every corner of Europe and Asia. From Africa negro slaves brought the matter of *Uncle Remus* to the American plantations; and in the remote South Seas, where the more genial four-footed beasts were unknown, the natives found entertainment in the colloquies of a lizard and a codfish. Nor is their appeal limited to children and simple folk; for Goethe retold the story of Reynard the Fox,[1] and Socrates occupied his last days in versifying the fables of Aesop.

The literary pedigree of the Nun's Priest's Tale begins with this Aesop, a Phrygian slave of the sixth century B.C. But the Greek fables that pass under his name are a miscellaneous collection of much later date, and they have little of the freshness one would expect from his legendary reputation. The fact is that Aesop's Fables became a school-book. They were revised, supplemented, versified, and translated by many imitators, some nameless, and some like Phaedrus, Babrius and Avianus, who are little more than names. Generations of schoolboys did exercises on them, retold them in prose, or turned them into verse; and it is no wonder they became trite with hard use. Anyhow, one of the best known of Aesop's Fables[2] gives us a starting-point, though it must not be

---

[1] *Reineke Fuchs*, 1794.
[2] In the edition of the Aesopic Fables by A. Chambry, Paris 1926, texts of this fable are given at pp. 285–7. It is referred to by Horace, *Satires* ii. v. 56; and it is the second fable of La Fontaine.

supposed that Chaucer's story derives from it in the direct line : we can only note the historical outcroppings of a theme whose main development is beyond the reach of records :

A Crow sitting in a tree and eating a piece of meat ('cheese' in another version) is approached by a hungry Fox, who praises its plumage and declares that it would be the first among birds if only it could sing. The Crow, much flattered, opens its beak to sing and drops the morsel, which the Fox snaps up.

This may seem remote from the tale of the Cock and the Fox, but the analogy becomes clearer when Chaucer's story is reduced to its framework of two similar tricks: (i) The Fox flatters the Cock into singing with eyes shut, so that he is caught; and (ii) the Cock flatters his captor into shouting back at the pursuers, and escapes as the Fox opens his mouth.[1]

In Western Europe Greek books were closed books throughout the Middle Ages, and Aesop's Fables were known chiefly through the medium of two Latin versifiers: Phaedrus, 'the freedman of Augustus', who wrote in the first century A. D., and Avianus, who belongs perhaps to the fourth century A. D.[2] For a time their collections were preserved by the lingering tradition of the Roman schools ; but they took on a new life in the eighth century, when Charles the Great gave his support to a revival of letters. The spirit of this revival (which was undertaken less for the sake of the classics themselves than as a necessary preliminary

---

[1] The attempt to connect our story with Aesop's fable of the Cock, Dog, and Fox is a failure. There is no historical contact, because this particular fable is omitted from the medieval collections ; and the stories are radically unlike. It explains nothing to say that Aesop's Dog, who is the Cock's guardian and kills the Fox, *develops* into 'Colle our dogge, and Talbot and Gerland ', who join a quite ineffective chase. Any farmyard cur would do that without needing an example in classical antiquity.

[2] Both edited, with their Latin derivatives, by L. Hervieux, *Les Fabulistes Latins,* 5 vols., Paris 1893–9.

to the study of the Bible and the Fathers) fostered the development of fables. If they were useful in the teaching of Latin, they were still more useful for the teaching of moral lessons; and from this time onwards the ' moral ', which is implied rather than expressed in the classical fables, became more and more prominent.

It so happens that while Avianus does not approach our story, and Phaedrus is content to hand on the fable of the Crow and the Fox, Alcuin of York (d. 804), who was Charles's right hand, carries us a step forward in his Latin verses on the Cock and the Wolf.[1]

A Cock, who ventures too far when looking for food, is caught by a Wolf. With great presence of mind, he mentions the report he has heard of the Wolf's wonderful voice, and says he does not mind being eaten so much as losing the chance of verifying this report. The Wolf opens wide his jaws to show off his voice, and the Cock, escaping to a high branch, chides him for his folly in shouting before he has dined.

This is, in essentials, the second trick.

Soon after Alcuin's time, Latin prose renderings of Phaedrus's verse eclipsed their original. By far the most influential of these is attributed to a shadowy Romulus, who is sometimes dignified by the title of ' Emperor ', though his empire does not extend beyond the realm of fable. This collection, made perhaps in the ninth century, and undergoing many modifications in the course of time, plays the chief part in the spread of fables during the later Middle Ages. But its direct contribution to our story is slight, for the early form of Romulus [2] seems to contain nothing more apposite than Phaedrus's version of the Crow and the Fox.

Another Latin prose version is more helpful. In

[1] Ed. Dümmler, *Monumenta Germaniae Historica: Poetae Aevi Carolini* i, p. 262.

[2] Several versions are printed and compared by Hervieux, *Les Fabulistes Latins,* vols. i and ii.

1034 Adhemar, a monk of the Abbey of St. Martial at Limoges, died in Jerusalem, whither he had gone some years before. One of the books he left behind at the Abbey included a collection of fables copied with his own hand, and it is now MS. Vossianus Latinus 8vo, no. 15 in the Leyden Library. This collection [1] consists in the main of crude adaptations from Phaedrus, among which is the Crow and the Fox. But it contains some fables found neither in Phaedrus nor in any other ancient source, and to this group belongs the Fox and the Partridge :

A Fox came up to a Partridge on her perch and said ' How beautiful are your face, your legs, your coral beak ! Yet you would look more beautiful still in your sleep.' The Partridge closed her eyes, and the Fox promptly seized her. The Partridge then implores the Fox to pronounce her name once more before he eats her, and when he opens his mouth to say ' Partridge ', she escapes. ' Alas ! ' says the Fox, ' what need had I to speak ? ' ' Alas ! ' replies the Partridge, ' what need had I to close my eyes when I wasn't sleepy '.

How Adhemar came by this story we do not know. But here is the eye-shutting trick played by a fox on a bird, together with the mouth-opening trick by which the tables are turned ; and the combination of old motives must have taken place before the year 1029, when Adhemar set out for the Holy Land.

The next record shows an advance in story-telling. The Brussels MS. 10708, fol. 172 [2] contains, in a hand that seems to be of the second half of the twelfth century, the Latin poem *Gallus et Vulpes*,[3] which was probably composed earlier in the same century :

A hungry Fox finds a Cock crowing on his dunghill and too

---

[1] Ed. Hervieux, ii, p. 142.

[2] I owe the identification of this MS. to the courtesy of the director of the Bibliothèque Royale, M. Paris.

[3] Printed in *Lateinische Gedichte des X. und XI. Jh.*, ed. J. Grimm and A. Schmeller, Göttingen 1838, p. 345 ff.

vigilant to be caught. So he tries flattery. 'Your father used to dance as he crew—perhaps you can't do that?' The Cock comes nearer, crowing and dancing giddily. 'Why', he asks, should I be thought a degenerate son?' 'Wonderful!' replies the Fox: 'your father lives again in you. But he used to shut his right eye.' 'I do the same', says the Cock, and adds that to his performance. The Fox falls flat, overcome with admiration. 'Who could believe it? You would even excel him if you shut both eyes.' The Cock does it, and is caught. Neighbours begin the chase, crying 'The Fox has got the Cock! Help, or the paragon of birds will perish!' The Fox is well away, when the Cock has a plan: 'Let my death be honourable. The pursuers say you have stolen me, and don't recognize your marvellous wit. Put me down and say "I am taking what is my own, not yours". Then I shall die happy.' The Fox carries out the suggestion and the Cock flies away. 'A plague on the unruly tongue!' cries the Fox. 'And a plague on the eyes that shut when they should see', says the Cock. A long religious interpretation follows.

To reach English soil we must leave Latin behind and follow the fable into vernacular literature. Towards the end of the twelfth century, Marie of France, who was one of the brilliant group of writers attached to the court of Henry II, wrote in French verse an *Ysopet* ('little Aesop') or collection of fables, which includes the following : [1]

My tale is of a Cock who stood on a dunghill and crew. A Fox came by and addressed him with smooth words: 'Sir,' he said, 'how handsome you are! I never saw so fine a bird! Your voice is surpassingly clear, and no bird ever sang better— saving your father whom I knew; but he crew better still because he shut his eyes.' 'I can do that,' says the Cock. He beats his wings and shuts his eyes tightly, thinking to crow more clarion clear. The Fox made a spring, seized him, and ran off towards the wood. The shepherds chased him across a field; the dogs barked all about him. 'There goes the Fox,' they cry, 'he has the Cock!' 'Come,' says the Cock, 'shout back to them that I am yours and you won't let me go.' The Fox tried to shout his loudest, and the Cock, slipping from his

---

[1] *Die Fabeln der Marie de France*, ed. Karl Warnke (Bibliotheca Normannica), Halle 1898, p. 198 ff.

mouth, flew into a high tree. The Fox, in his rage, began to
curse the mouth that speaks when it should be still. 'And I',
replied the Cock, 'have cause to curse the eye that winks when
it should keep watch and ward against harm that may come
upon its master.'

In her Prologue Marie mentions 'Romulus the
Emperor', and most of her stories come from Romulus,

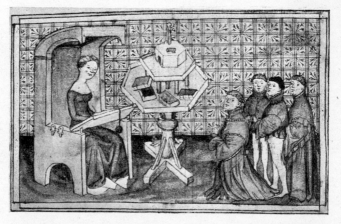

Marie of France reading her poems.

though this particular one does not.[1] In an Epilogue
she gives a more circumstantial account of her sources :
Aesop translated the fables from Greek into Latin ;
King Alfred, who liked them well, turned them into
English ; and Marie herself turned them from English
into French verse. Now it is as certain that King
Alfred did not translate the fables into English as
that Aesop did not translate them into Latin.[2] But

---

[1] It occurs in the 'Anglo-Latin Romulus' (Hervieux, ii, p. 598) ;
but there it appears to be derived from Marie.

[2] In the twelfth century Alfred's reputation for wisdom stood high,
and another popular compilation of the time, the 'Proverbs of Alfred',
is attributed to him on no better grounds.

Marie's testimony carries more weight when she says she translated from English. Either this is mere literary mystification (improbable, though not impossible in the century of Geoffrey of Monmouth) or there was once a fable collection in English which has been wholly lost. And as there is slight internal evidence in support of Marie's statement, the latter alternative should be preferred.[1] Did this English version contain our story as it appears in Marie? We do not know, and even if we could prove that it did, we should not be much the wiser. The source of the details in her version, and in *Gallus et Vulpes* before it, seems to be the story of Reynard the Fox as it grew up in France during the twelfth century.

II. REYNARD THE FOX.

The twelfth century stands out as a lively and creative age in Western Europe, whether it is judged by great movements (such as the rise of a new architecture, of universities, of a multitude of new literary forms and kinds in the vernacular) or by its results in some tiny detail, as when it gives new life to the dry bones of a fable that had been chewed unprofitably for centuries before. What happy combination of circumstances unlocked this abounding vitality it is impossible to say. But one aspect is suggested by the history we have just traced. Preceding ages had always before them the model of Rome in her days of greatness. Those who cared for literature imitated the Latin classics; and by using a dead language and the forms and subjects of a past civilization, they cut

[1] See a valuable article by E. Mall in *Zeitschrift für romanische Philologie*, vol. ix.

themselves off from the mass of the people. Once it was realized that an author could express the things that interested his contemporaries in his own language and in the forms that suited it, expression led with amazing swiftness to fuller and better expression. A literature arose that was popular in the sense that the whole people—nobles, clergy, traders, artisans, peasants —could share in it ; for while works (other than learned works) circulated orally rather than by the medium of books, inability to read was not a bar to the enjoyment of poetry, and inability to write did not prevent a man who had something worth telling from adding it to the common stock.

There is a change, too, in the purpose of authors. For many centuries the view of the Church that literature should instruct had prevailed against the example of the classics ; but now, with the growth of a minstrel class who lived by catering for the varied tastes of the people, a considerable number of works appear which have no other object than entertainment.

One more change concerns us closely : a new interest in natural things, particularly in birds and animals, is a sign of the break with the past. Granted that they fell far short of modern precision and range of observation, that they soon relapsed into convention, and that their curiosity was easily satisfied by absurdities such as those reported in *Physiologus* and the derived Bestiaries ; still writers of the twelfth and thirteenth centuries give ample evidence of a fresh and sympathetic outlook on nature, which finds expression too in painting and the ornaments of architecture.

These are some of the conditions under which the cycle of animal stories grew up that bears the name of Reynard the Fox, its principal character ; and they are not satisfied by the old fables in which a Partridge, a Fox, a Cock, play their parts with the dispassionate efficiency of the points *A*, *B*, *C* in a proposition of Euclid. In the French 'beast epic' a fresh draft on the memory and imagination of the people produces many stories new to literature, as well as variations of the old ; the animals are described in their own shapes and with their own habits, but whimsical effects are obtained by giving them the thoughts and speech of men ; they are no longer types, but have character and 'personality'; and they have proper names, some of which have a claim to immortality : men's names like *Reynard*[1] the Fox, *Isengrim* the Wolf, *Bruin* the Bear, *Tibert* the Cat ; or descriptive names like *Chantecler* the ' clear-voiced' Cock, *Couart* the ' timid' Hare, *Noble* the Lion.

The first trace of the cycle in history is a mention of Isengrim by Guibert de Nogent (d. *circa* 1125) :— Waldric, Bishop of Laon, was accustomed to give a villainous-looking fellow called Teudegald the nickname *Isengrim*, ' because of his wolfish face '. It seems to have rankled, for Teudegald recalled the insult when he found the Bishop hiding in a cask in the cellar of his church, and beat him unmercifully.[2] This was in the year 1112.

Isengrim the Wolf is again prominent in the earliest surviving treatment of the cycle—the Latin poem *Ysengrimus*,[3] written by Nivard in the year 1148, probably at Ghent. Nivard is so far old-fashioned that he uses the animal stories to point a heavy satire

---

[1] In French *renard* has become the common name of the fox. Like all men's names in the cycle, it is German in origin, Old High German *Reginhart*, ' the very bold ' ; for at this time Frankish proper names were usual in France. But Gaston Paris has suggested that the cycle arose on the borders of the Rhine, for the personal name *Isengrim*, ' iron-mask ', is not recorded west of Lorraine, and some minor names have similar geographical limits.

[2] Migne, *Patrologia Latina*, vol. clvi, col. 927 f.

[3] Edited by Ernst Voigt, Halle 1884.

against corruption in the religious orders; but his poem proves the existence of a connected series of tales; and among them, at the end of the Fourth Book, appears the story of Reynard the Fox and the Cock, who is called *Sprotinus*, probably because the name *Chantecler* was not yet fixed in tradition.

Sprotinus is lord of a dozen hens, and proud of his crowing. Reynard comes in the dress of a pilgrim, and though the Cock is suspicious, induces him by taunts to follow the example of his father and to crow, first standing on one leg with one eye shut, then with both eyes shut. Reynard grabs him; the rustics give chase; the Cock persuades him to shout back defiance, and escapes from his jaws, leaving him to curse his foolish mouth.

Thirty or forty years after Nivard's *Ysengrimus*, an Alsatian, Heinrich Glichezare, wrote his *Reinhart Fuchs*,[1] a German poem of some 2,000 lines, which recounts the principal episodes of the Reynard cycle, beginning with the story of Reynard and Chantecler. Heinrich's *Reinhart* is in the main a translation and abridgement of French originals; but it is important because for the first time it tells the tales without any didactic purpose, and because it is earlier, and in some respects more primitive, than any extant French version. In the part that concerns us, *Reinhart Fuchs* is much nearer to Chaucer than the works noticed hitherto; but as it cannot be proved that Chaucer used a version nearer in any significant detail to Heinrich's poem than to the French *Roman de Renard*,[2] whereas the converse is true in some points, we may pass on at once to the French *Roman*.

The *Roman de Renard*[3] is a collection of over twenty 'branches', composed (for the most part) in the north of France by various poets of the late twelfth and early thirteenth centuries. Each branch tells a story or a connected group of stories, but there

---

[1] Edited by K. Reissenberger, Halle 1886.
[2] See § III below. [3] Ed. E. Martin, Strasbourg 1882–7.

is no ordered sequence of branches : the *Roman* grew
up, and was not built to a design. Its kernel seems
to be the story of the quarrel between Reynard and
Ysengrim. Upon this the adventures of Reynard with
other animals were easily grafted ; and finally some
episodes were added in which Reynard is not concerned. Thus the whole work is a loosely assembled
body of animal tales in verse, saved from complete
incoherence by the presiding genius of Reynard, and
by the common desire of the authors to ' give delight
and hurt not '.[1]

The Second Branch, which alone concerns us, is a
favourable specimen. After a prologue which promises
the story of the war between the barons Reynard and
Ysengrim, it begins with Reynard and Chantecler, to
whom we shall return. Disconsolate at the loss of his
dinner, Reynard meets the Tomtit and varies the old
trick, promising to shut his eyes while the Tomtit
kisses him ; but the Tomtit evades his snap and pushes
a handful of moss into his mouth. Next he finds
Tibert the Cat alone at play, frisking and chasing his
tail ; and from sheer malice devises a sport that will
lead Tibert into a trap. Tibert, however, notices the
trap, and hounds coming up unexpectedly drive Reynard himself into it. He escapes with a mangled paw,
and comes upon Tiecelin the Crow, who is gulping
down a cheese he has stolen from an old woman.
Reynard persuades him to sing in the manner of his

---

[1] It is often said that an idea underlies all the adventures of Reynard
—that his guile succeeds against the strong (e.g. Ysengrim or Bruin)
and fails against the weak (e.g. Chantecler). This is an uncon-
sidered result, not a motive. Reynard does succeed against the
weak when his object is not to kill : he gets the cheese from Tiecelin
the Crow. He fails when his desire is to kill, and the stronger animals
fail against him, because the medieval story-tellers were skilled enough
in their art to know that it is unwise to dispose of the characters while
the story is still popular, and that amusement is not easily extracted from
the destruction of the weak by the strong.

father Rohart; and after two trials declares that he
would be the finest singer in the world if only he would
avoid nuts in his diet.   'One more try,' he begs, and

Reynard and Tiecelin.

in a last effort Tiecelin lets the cheese slip from his
claws.[1] After these diversions Reynard carries on the
war, which is his main business, by playing an impu-
dent trick on Ysengrim.

[1] Note that the compiler of this branch recognized the kinship of the
Crow story and the Cock story, and assimilated them by making the
Crow, too, sing after the model of his father. In Branch ix, l. 570,
there is a further assimilation: Tiecelin's father is called Chanteclin
('he who sings with closed eyes'), which is the name of Chantecler's father.

Now that we have seen what the branch contains, let us turn back to its first story, and, for convenience, deal with some 450 lines of the French by a mixture of translation, paraphrase, and abridgement :—

Reynard makes his way to a village in a wood, where there are many cocks and hens, geese and ducks. His special object is a favourite spot of his—the yard of a rich farmer, Constant des Noes, who is abundantly stocked with poultry, salt meat and bacon, good cherries and apples. The yard is well fenced with oak palings and thorn hurdles ; and Reynard can find no way through. Yet he knows that if he jumps over, the hens will see him, and run for shelter under the thorns. At last he finds a broken paling, slips over, and hides among the cabbages. But the hens catch sight of him and run for safety.

Their flurry rouses Chantecler, who is enjoying a dust-bath in a track near the wood, and he walks proudly in, stretching his neck and trailing his wings, to inquire why they ran to the house. His favourite Pinte, 'she who laid the big eggs ', replies 'We were frightened '. 'Why? what did you see?' ' Some wild beast who would harm us if we did not take shelter.' 'It's nothing, I'll swear,' said the Cock. ' Don't be afraid ; you're quite safe here.' ' But I saw it this very minute,' Pinte insisted. ' Saw what ? ' ' I saw the fence shake and the cabbage leaves tremble where it lies.' ' Pinte,' said the Cock, ' no more of this. No fox or polecat would dare come into this yard. A mere illusion, my dear, I assure you ; so come back.' And back he went himself to his dust-bath, and there settled down, one eye open and one shut, one leg outstretched, the other doubled up.

Wearied of watching and crowing, he slept, and dreamed that there was something in the yard clad in a red fur-coat fringed with bone ; and it thrust the coat upon him to his great discomfort, for the collar was very tight. He starts up in terror: ' Holy Spirit,' he prays, ' save my body from prison this day and keep me safe ' ; and then, all his assurance gone, runs to where the hens are hiding under the thorns, and tells Pinte that he is in great dread of some wild beast or bird. ' Avoy ! sweet sir,' says Pinte, ' you must not talk like that and frighten us so. By all the saints, you are like a dog that howls before the stone hits him ! Why are you so frightened ? ' ' I have had a strange dream ', answers the Cock, ' and an ill-omened ! That is why you see me so pale. I shall tell you every detail '—(and he goes on to tell of the beast with the red fur-coat). ' Do you know what it signifies?' 'Please God it turn out false!' says Pinte, 'but I can interpret it. The beast with the red fur-coat is the Fox; the fringe of bone is his teeth; the tight collar his mouth', &c., 'and he will get you by the neck before mid-day is past. I advise you to come back, for I know he is lying in wait for you behind that clump of cabbages.' 'Pinte,' said he, 'this is folly, and it is unworthy of you to say that the beast is in this yard who shall take me by force. Curse him who believes it! for I won't believe this dream portends any harm to me.' 'God grant it may be so,' replied Pinte, 'yet if what I say is false, let me be no more your love.'

Chantecler laughs off the dream, goes back to his dust-bath, and begins to doze again. When he has settled down, Reynard creeps nearer, makes a spring, misses, and sees Chantecler jump to safety on the dunghill. Reynard is chagrined, but immediately sets his brain to work. 'Don't run away, Chantecler,' he cries, 'it is I, your own cousin.' Chantecler crew with relief. 'Do you remember your father Chanteclin?' asks Reynard. 'No cock ever crew like him: one could hear him a league away when he crew with both eyes shut.' 'You aren't trying to trick me, cousin Reynard?' asks Chantecler. 'Indeed no! Try crowing with your eyes shut. We are one flesh and blood, and I would rather lose a paw than see you harmed.' 'I don't believe you,' says Chantecler, 'so please stand a little farther off, and I will crow for you.' 'A high note, then!' says Reynard, smiling. Chantecler crew once, with one eye shut and the other open, for he was suspicious of Reynard, and often looked his way. 'That's nothing,' says Reynard, 'Chanteclin did not crow like that. He shut both eyes and held his note so that he could be heard twenty fields away.' Chantecler, convinced, shuts both eyes to crow. At once Reynard jumps out from under a red cabbage, seizes him by the neck, and off he goes delighted with his prize.

Pinte is beside herself with grief at the sight: 'Sir, now my warning proves true, and you laughed at me and called me a fool! Your pride was your ruin! Alas! I die of grief, for if I lose my lord I lose my honour for ever!'

The good wife opened the door, for it was evening, and called in Pinte, Rosette, and Bise, but no hen came. Then, as she called the Cock loudly, she saw Reynard going off with him, and went to the rescue. Reynard increased his pace, and when she saw she could not catch him, she gave the alarm with a full-throated 'Harrow!' The farm-hands ran to find out what was the matter. 'Alas!' she said, 'disaster has come upon me.'

' How ? ' ' I have lost my Cock—the Fox has taken him.'
' Old slattern ! ' cried Constant, ' why didn't you catch the Fox ? '
' By all the saints, I couldn't.' ' Why not ? ' ' He wouldn't wait
for me.' ' But you could hit him ? ' ' What with ? ' ' With this
stick.' ' Indeed I couldn't: he ran so fast that two Breton hounds

The Chase.

couldn't have caught him.' ' Which way ? ' ' That way, just
there.' The farm-hands ran shouting ' There he is ! There he is !'
Just then Reynard reached the opening and jumped down with
such a thud that the pursuers heard him. ' There he is ! There he
is ! ' they cry. ' After him,' shouts Constant, and calls his dog
Mauvoisin. ' After him, Bardolph, Travers, Humbaut, Rebors ! '
They get sight of Reynard, and shout ' There goes the Fox '.

Now Chantecler is in great peril, and needs all his wits.

'Reynard,' he says, ' can't you hear the insults these men are
shouting at you ? When Constant shouts " Reynard has him "
why not mock him by answering " in your despite " ? ' Reynard's
cunning for once was at fault. ' In your despite ! ' he yelled, and
as the Cock felt his jaws relax, he beat his wings, and flew into
an apple-tree. Then he laughed at Reynard, who stood below
disgusted at his own folly : ' Reynard,' he said, ' what do you
think of it all ? ' Reynard quivered with rage : ' Cursed be the
mouth ', he said, ' that makes a noise when it should be silent.'
' And ', says the Cock, ' I say a plague on the eyes that sleep
when they ought to keep watch ! ' Then Chantecler rates
Reynard for his perfidy and bids him be off before he loses his
skin. Reynard runs on dejected at the loss of his dinner.

This is the *Roman de Renard* at its best. The
subsequent history of the cycle in France is one of
rapid decline in the hands of didactic writers, who
represent Reynard as the embodiment of evil, and
gradually crush the gaiety out of his adventures by
loading them with crude satire, or moral lessons, or
still less relevant instruction.[1] Before the end of the
fourteenth century the subject was exhausted and discarded in French literature. Probably the best of the
separate stories were repeated until they sank back
to the level of folk tales ; but the cycle lived on
in European literature through an early thirteenth-
century Flemish version,[2] which spread eastward into
Germany to be the basis of *Reineke Fuchs* (Goethe's

---

[1] The three later French versions are :

   (i) *Le Couronnement Renard*, written soon after 1250, in which
Reynard, who is the type of successful hypocrisy and wickedness,
succeeds the Lion as King of the Beasts.

   (ii) *Renard le Nouveau*, written by Gelée of Lille about 1300,
which tells of the unsuccessful war of Noble the Lion, representing
Virtue, against Reynard, representing Vice.

   (iii) *Renard le Contrefait* (ed. G. Raynaud and H. Lemaître, Paris
1914), written at Troyes early in the fourteenth century by a merchant
who had been a clerk. Here satire and morality are combined with all
manner of irrelevant information.

[2] *Van den Vos Reinaerde*, ed. E. Martin, Paderborn, 1874.

original) and westward into England as Caxton's *His-
torye of Reynart the Foxe*.[1]

III. CHAUCER'S TREATMENT.

The tracing of sources is chiefly valuable because it
shows how deeply Chaucer's work is rooted in the
past. But if any one hopes to account for all the
details of his version by long hunting among his pre-
decessors, it is a vain hope. Invention usually baffles
this kind of investigation, and it is seldom possible to
do more with safety than say that a turn or incident is
in this text and not in that. To go further and explain
the relations between two texts, such as the *Renard*
story and the Nun's Priest's Tale, involves a good deal
of conjecture.

At the outset some questions suggest themselves.
(i) Did Chaucer know the *Roman de Renard*? Observe
the difference in the names : Chantecler, Pinte, Renard,
in the *Roman* ; Chantecler, Pertelote, Russell, in
Chaucer. That Pinte should take another French
name is perhaps not very important, though it is a
break with well-established tradition. But it is no
small matter that the famous Reynard, whom the
imagination of French poets a century before had
raised to the lordship of the world, should be given
a mere descriptive name *Russell* 'the red ',[2] which in

---

[1] 'I have not added ne mynusshed (diminished), but have folowed as
nyghe as I can my copye whiche was in Dutche, and by me William
Caxton translated into this rude and symple Englyssh, in th'abbey of
Westmestre fynysshed the vi daye of Juyn, the yere of our lord
MCCCCLXXXI.' From the Epilogue, ed. Arber, London 1880.

[2] *Russell* is the name of one of Reynard's children in Caxton's version
from the Flemish. But there is no reason to think that Chaucer (or a
predecessor) borrowed the name, which is an obvious one for a red
thing or person.

the *Roman* belongs to the obscure red squirrel.   The
substitution is hardly credible if Chaucer took his
matter directly from the Reynard cycle : it indicates
that his source was a story detached from the cycle,
in which Chantecler had become the chief actor, and
Reynard, stripped of his personality and the prestige
of his other exploits, had sunk back to be just a wily
fox.   Then it would be natural enough for Chaucer to
give the fox a current name with no literary traditions
behind it, like ' Colle oure dogge ' and the ' sheep that
highte Malle '.   And Pinte, too, may have become
anonymous before she attained to the dignity of
' Madame Pertelote '.[1]

This indication is confirmed when we find that
Chaucer only once in his works names Reynard, and
there it is a common name for the fox.[2] He does not
refer to any other incident in the *Roman de Renard*.
And the case is the same with the two great contemporary poems—*Piers Plowman* and Gower's *Confessio Amantis*—in which the authors had opportunity
to mention anything that was much in their thoughts.
It is hard to resist the conclusion that the Reynard
cycle had gone out of fashion in England, as it had in
France, by the latter half of the fourteenth century.[3]
The separate stories may have lived on ; and though
there is not much doubt that all were told in England

[1] ' It is ful faire to been y-clept *Madame* ', and more honour still to
give a name to a long line of partlets.

[2] *Legend of Good Women*, l. 2448.

[3] The representations in carving require further investigation ; but
where several scenes of the Reynard story appear, e.g. at Bristol, the
subjects and the late date indicate that they derive from Caxton's version.
Some late fourteenth-century and early fifteenth-century carvings have
a goose instead of a cock, which shows that their relation with the
Roman de Renard is not close.   It is worth noting that the distaff which
appears in Chaucer l. 618, in *The False Fox* (note to l. 569), in all the
carvings of the chase, and in some illustrations of the *Roman* (e.g.
that reproduced at p. xxi), is not specified in the *Roman* itself, nor
is there a trace of it in the other literary versions.

at one time or another, it happens that the cycle is
represented in the extant remains of Middle English
by two stories only—the thirteenth-century *Fox and
Wolf*[1] and Chaucer's Nun's Priest's Tale. Caxton,
as we have seen, had to go to Flanders for his *Reynard
the Fox*. Chaucer may never have known the cycle
as a whole.

(ii) What was the language of Chaucer's source?
The evidence for a French original is clear: *Avoi!*
cries Pinte in the *Roman* when Chantecler says he is
frightened by his dream, and *Avoy!* cries Pertelote
at the same place (l. 142) : the word is not used elsewhere in Chaucer. The Fox shouts *Maugre vostre*
at his pursuers in the *Roman*, and *Maugree youre heed!*
in Chaucer (l. 646). But it is not possible to say
whether these phrases come to Chaucer direct from
French, or whether they were transmitted through an
English intermediary, for both are found earlier in
Middle English.[2]

(iii) Is the ultimate source the *Roman de Renard*
or some other French version? That Chaucer takes
his story from a version identical with the *Roman* in
some details of phrasing appears from the examples
just quoted, and from the Cock's prayer after his
dream, where the *Roman* has *Seint Esperiz, Garis hui
mon cors de prison* = ' God . . . Kepe my body out of
foul prisoun ' (l. 130 f.). But in the broader lines of
treatment Chaucer is sometimes nearer to Heinrich
Glichezare and Marie de France. For example, the
Fox's first spring, which spoils the story by giving
Chantecler full warning of Reynard's purpose, is

---

[1] Often printed, e.g. in *Middle English Humorous Tales*, ed.
G. H. McKnight, Boston 1913.

[2] *harrow*, one of three exclamations in l. 614, is paralleled by *harou*
in the *Roman*, but the expression is too common in French and Middle
English to have any value as evidence of relation.

peculiar to the *Roman,* and it has been shown[1] that
it is an interpolation from another branch of the cycle.
The absence of this incident in Chaucer might seem
at first sight to be evidence that he used a version
more primitive in this respect than the *Roman.* But
it is the kind of detail that Chaucer himself, or an
intermediary, would discard, just as Chantecler's
crowing first with one eye shut is discarded, though it
is proved to be primitive by *Gallus et Vulpes* and
Nivard's *Ysengrimus.* Any shortening of the *Roman*
version, in which the action is most fully developed,
must tend to approach the simpler early forms by
the dropping of less essential incidents. It cannot be
proved by comparison with other versions that the
Nun's Priest's Tale is not in the direct line of descent
from the *Roman de Renard*; and as the likeness of
phrasing is easiest explained by assuming a direct line
of descent, that assumption should be preferred.[2]

(iv) Our first deduction—that Chaucer did not take
his story directly from the *Roman,* and our third—
that it is in the direct line of descent from the *Roman,*
raise the question of lost intermediate versions. It is
impossible to make a useful guess at their number,
which (in the absence of evidence) might be two or
twenty. But it is unlikely that all the lost inter-
mediaries were written. No scribe or editor, and
certainly no poet of Chaucer's ability, would have
sacrificed so many of the good things of the *Roman* if
he had had them before him in writing. A stage of
oral tradition, in which the text might suffer from
faults of memory or from the limits of time imposed
on the story-teller, will best account for the shortening

[1] By Voretzsch, *Zeitschrift für romanische Philologie,* vol. xv (1891),
pp. 136 ff. A valuable article. [2] Miss Petersen *On the Sources,*
&c., assumes a lost source combining features from the *Roman* and from
Heinrich Glichezare, but her conclusions are pushed too far.

and simplification of the plot; for the change or dis-
appearance of important proper names; the faithful
preservation of trivial phrases uttered at critical
moments; and the loss of literary finish—all of which
may reasonably be assumed in Chaucer's immediate
source, whether that source was oral or written.

Other divergences fit well enough with these conclusions. In the *Roman* Pinte warns Chantecler that
his dream means immediate danger, and he laughs at
her fears; in Chaucer he is afraid of his dream and
she laughs at him, putting her faith in the herbs which
he scorns. Here the essential thing for the story is
the domestic difference of opinion: the sides taken do
not matter so much. But in the *Roman* Chantecler is
at first afraid and Pinte is derisive ('You are like the
dog that howls before the stone hits him'); and
derived versions, or even Chaucer himself, whose
sympathies as between husband and wife are not in
doubt, might well choose to develop the argument
along these lines.

Then, again, in the *Roman* there is an elaborate
account of the farm of Constant de Noes, of the
arrangements for keeping Reynard out of this fox's
paradise, and his successful entry. In Chaucer a poor
widow owns the yard. There is no need to suppose
that Chaucer metamorphosed the rich farmer into the
poor widow. In the shortening of the story when it
was separated from the cycle, the name of Constant
de Noes would naturally disappear, together with the
details of Reynard's approach. But at the starting of
the chase the farmer's wife must be prominent, as she
is in the *Roman*, however much the story is cut down.
Even the carvings of the scene find room for her.
From this part of the tale Chaucer (or an intermediary) would assume that she was the owner of the
yard and the Cock.

This leads to the last point we need notice : In the
Roman attention is focussed on Reynard from the
beginning, and all his movements are minutely
recorded.   In Chaucer he does not appear at all till
the tale is half told.   This is what we should expect.
The *Roman* is the *Roman de Renard,* and each of its
stories is told as an episode in his career.   But when
one of them is detached from its setting, Reynard
loses in importance.   The centre of interest shifts, and
the Nun's Priest justly says ' My tale is of a Cok '.

We have lingered over the plot ; yet on a strict
reckoning it takes up barely a fifth of Chaucer's
narrative.   His own work appears most in the em-
broidering by which he made an old story new.   He
begins with a description of the poor widow and her
household (55–80), which is as sharp as any in the
Prologue, and is unmistakably his own.   Her humble
roof supplies the perch for the more brilliant household of a prince among cocks, and the description of
Chantecler and his wives (81–115) brings us closer to
the matter.   With Chantecler's dream (116–41), which
includes a miniature portrait of the Fox, all the
characters are introduced, and the story begins in
earnest.   But almost immediately Madame Pertelote
strays into considerations on the ideal husband (145–
51) ;   and then she launches the subject of dreams
and their medical aspects (155–203).   Chantecler
refutes her by the stock examples : two dream stories
taken ultimately from Cicero (218–338) with a minor
digression on the theme ' Murder will out ' (284–91) ;
St.   Kenelm (344–55) ;   Scipio's Dream (356–60) ;
Daniel, Joseph, Pharaoh (361–9) ; Croesus and Andromache (370–82)—till dawn, calling him to his duty,
brings relief (383 f.).   Not till l. 406 does he fly down
from his perch, and it takes some dozen lines more

(421–33) to bring out the date of the fatal morning, and its astrological significance.[1]

At the close of his argument he had felt something of the melancholy grandeur of doomed Hector; but Pertelote's beauty (394–6) banishes his fears. He turns the ominous ' Mulier est hominis confusio ' to a jest; and the spring day (434–7) raises him to the height of joy which goes before tragedy. Hence some reflections on 'ever the latter end of joy is woe' (439–43), followed by an assurance that the story is true (444–7), and a promise to get on with it (448), which is fulfilled when the Fox is introduced into the yard (449–57), like the Serpent into Eden (cp. l. 492). But only eight lines are spared for the story proper. Famous traitors—Judas Iscariot, Ganelon, Sinon—are brought to mind (461–3); the evil day is cursed (464–7); a promising excursus on predestination is begun (468–84), only to be dismissed as irrelevant to the ' tale of a Cok '; and the folly of taking women's advice is exposed (490–500). Then for a while the tale goes on smoothly: there are brief asides on mermaids (505 f.) and on natural antipathies (513–15), but the Fox in his long speech (518–55) sticks to the point unswervingly, speaking not a word in vain, and falling into reminiscence only to tell of a cock that was very ingenious, yet not comparable in discretion with Chantecler's father who crew with both eyes shut. Chantecler beats his wings to crow, but before he can rise on his toes six lines on flattery are interpolated (559–64), and his capture opens the floodgates of digression : there is an appeal to Destiny, another to Venus, a dig at Geoffrey de Vinsauf's chiding of ' the Friday' (572–88); the classical scenes of women's

---

[1] May 3 is one of the ' Egyptian days ', or *dies mali*, on which it is dangerous to undertake anything. The day was the unlucky Friday, Venus's day, and the sun was in Taurus, the ' house' of Venus.

wailing are recalled (589–607); and still another promise is given to return to the story. And now, with fully half the action untold and a tenth of his time left, Chaucer fulfils his promise: from the moment the widow starts the chase till the moral ends the tale, there is no pause.

No evidence suggests that Chaucer found these diversions in his immediate source: they appear to be his own contribution to the story. And they serve one general purpose. The great scene in the tale of the Cock and the Fox, as we know from book-illustrations and carvings, and, indeed, from Chaucer's own treatment, is the scurrying chase that turns a peaceful farmyard into pandemonium; and he deliberately holds back this scene, approaching it as slowly and indirectly as his audience will permit. For he is both entertaining them and teasing them with suspense and irrelevance: he keeps an eye on them all the time, gauging to a nicety how far he can go without spoiling their pleasure, cajoling them with a promise [1] or muffling a protest by protesting first.[2] But when once the chase is started, his burst of pace is all the more effective by contrast. A score of verses (611–35) are crowded with noise and action, and nothing is allowed to drag afterwards: even the moral, which at an earlier stage might have given rise to long discussion, is dispatched in two business-like lines (670 f.).

If now we compare Chaucer's additions with the handling of the same plot in the *Roman de Renard*, a notable difference appears. The *Roman* version rattles along, almost without reflections and digressions; there is plenty of lively detail, but it springs naturally out of the action, and there is no clear-cut distinction

---

[1] But I wol passe as lightly as I kan, 173; And after wol I telle his áventùre, 420; Now wol I torne agayn to my senténce, 448; cp. 608.

[2] I wol nat han to do of swich matéere,—
My tale is of a Cok, as ye may heere. ll. 485 f.

between the story itself and the divagations from it. This is not a difference between two individual poets, or two nations : the same tendency for description, discussion, and moralizing comment to grow till they clog the story, may be seen if a fourteenth-century English romance is compared with one of the early thirteenth century, or if the late French *Renard le Contrefait* is set beside the *Roman de Renard.* In fact, description and digression were the vices of narrative in Chaucer's day. He made description one of the chief merits of his poetry by freeing it of convention and using it with masterly restraint ; but though he knew the dangers well enough, he was too much a man of his time to escape altogether from the snares of digression.

It may be said that in the Nun's Priest's Tale he is laughing at this literary vice, and in a sense that is true. But it is an unusual kind of laughter. For there is little doubt that some such interpolations, taken seriously, were to the taste of his audience, so that they must laugh at themselves. And there is a further complexity : Chaucer liked them. The long excursus on dreams is paralleled by the serious argument in Troilus v, 358–85 ; predestination is dragged into Troilus iv, 961 ff., with no artistic excuse ; and the Franklin's Tale is marred for modern readers by the citation of Hasdrubal's wife and other classical parallels (F. 1367–1456) after the manner of ll. 589 ff. So in these digressions Chaucer is indulging his inclination and laughing at himself too. And this is one of the attractions of his work. A man who is in part his own butt is not likely to be a savage and uncomfortable satirist ; and a man who can look at things from so many sides that he sees the ridiculous in himself will be a tolerant and easy companion ; though if he is very self-conscious, as Chaucer was, too keen a sense of the ridiculous may cumber him in the higher flights of poetry. Besides, there is a fascination in trying to follow the thoughts of such a Proteus, where the chances of being deluded are high. Do ll. 581 ff., for instance, mean simply that he had a good-natured contempt for Geoffrey de Vinsauf, or may we read between the lines that he had studied the *Nova Poetria* seriously as part of his training in the art of poetry, and that it still had a place in his uncritical affections? To know for certain when he is wholly in earnest and when he writes wholly in fun is the hardest problem that Chaucer has left to his readers.

In what has just been said, it is assumed that Chaucer is not laughing at his own views and practices because he has outgrown them, but because he is in the mood for laughing; and on this assumption we cannot infer that the Nun's Priest's Tale is necessarily later than other works (like *Troilus*) whose weaknesses it seems to expose. Nor can a certain conclusion as to the date of composition be drawn from the indications that the tale was not specially written for its present place in the series.[1] There is no satisfactory evidence that fixes the date within the obvious limits established by Chaucer's death in 1400, and by a casual reference to the massacre of Flemings in June 1381 (ll. 628 ff.).[2] But at least we may be sure that it was written in a happy time—not necessarily a time of posts and pensions, or even of good bodily health, but one in which he felt his powers at the full. The whimsical

---

[1] See p. xli below, and the notes to ll. 372, 604 f. The opposite view, that the main story and some of its digressions belong to the type of *exempla*, or sermon stories, and are therefore specially fitted to a priest, is not well founded, for a very large proportion of medieval stories are *exempla*.

[2] See the Notes, p. 57. It is almost the only sign of the stirring times in which he lived that Chaucer allows to appear in the *Canterbury Tales*.

subject called for all his subtlety. He had to keep
a nice balance between the natural characters of the
animals and their human attributes, for on the clash
and blending of these much of the humour depends.
Where the whole machinery of mock-heroic treatment
would be too artificial, and the simple story of a farmyard incident too plain, he had to combine the interests
of both. If the mock-heroical element gave him an
opportunity to display his curious learning, it was on
condition that he also displayed its vanity. Above all,
he must resist the temptation to fall into serious satire,
which would break the fantasy. He succeeded, where
so many failed, by serene good temper as well as art,
and it is this that makes the Nun's Priest's Tale the
favourite of most readers of *The Canterbury Tales.*

IV. THE SETTING

It remains to see how Chaucer gave the story a new
setting in *The Canterbury Tales,* which he designed to
be no mere collection, but an organized work : the
tales are pulled together, so that their several merits
may be enhanced, by a frame describing the Canterbury pilgrims and the course of their story-telling,
which comprises the Prologue ; the preambles of the
Wife of Bath, Pardoner, and Canon's Yeoman ; the
links between tales ; and the ' Retracciouns '[1] at
the end.

When he took this project in hand, about the year
1386, Chaucer had some stories by him which he could
adapt ;[2] but he intended to write many more, and his

---

[1] See the note to l. 679 (ii).

[2] The Second Nun's Tale of St. Cecilia is a clear instance ; it is
a separate story which Chaucer refers to in the Prologue to the *Legend
of Good Women,* and it is not adapted at all to the teller. There is
a prayer to those ' that reden that I write ', and the ' I ' is elsewhere
described as ' unworthy sone of Eve '.

C

first plan was a spacious one. It is outlined by the
Host when the pilgrims are assembled at the Tabard
Inn, Southwark, the night before they start for Can-
terbury:

> Ech of yow, to shorté with oure weye,
> In this viáge shal tellé tales tweye,—
> To Caunterbury-ward, I mene it so,
> And homward he shal tellen othere two,—
> Of áventùres that whilom han bifalle:
> And which of yow that bereth hym best of alle,
> That is to seyn, that telleth in this caas
> Tales of best senténce and moost soláas,
> Shal have a soper at oure aller cost,
> Heere in this placè, sittynge by this post,
> Whan that we come agayn fro Caunterbury.

As there were 'wel nine and twenty'[1] in the company besides our Host of the Tabard, and Chaucer
himself, who was to be a story-teller as well as the
reporter for all, this plan would call for one hundred
and twenty-four tales, if the Canon and his Yeoman,
who first joined the party at Boughton-under-Blean, are
left out of the count. But Chaucer found the task too
heavy, and shortened his plan to one tale apiece on
the outward journey; for when Canterbury is near, the
Host calls on the Parson, saying:

> Now lakketh us no tales mo than oon . . .
> For every man save thou hath told his tale.

The Parson agrees to

>   'telle a myrie tale in prose
> To knytte up al this feeste and make an ende';

and as soon as it is told, the author takes leave in his
'Retracciouns'.

Even on this reduced scale the work was not finished.
Only twenty complete tales are told, including the
Canon's Yeoman's. Two more break off abruptly
without explanation: the Cook barely begins his tale

---

[1] In fact thirty are mentioned in the Prologue.

of Perkin Revelour,[1] and the Squire 'leaves half-told
the story of Cambuskan bold'. Two more, Chaucer's
own *Sir Thopas* and the Monk's Tale,[2] are stopped
by the Host and the Knight. And Chaucer had not
so far decided on the tales that were to fill the gaps,
and the manner of their treatment, as to supply the
links which would have made the arrangement certain.
There are several loose ends—tales that are not linked
to anything before them, like the Man of Law's, or
tales that are not linked to anything following, like
the Nun's Priest's. Whether Death, 'the privy thief',
came upon him unawares, or whether the zest or
inspiration went from him before he died, he seems to
have left behind a bundle of manuscript, partly finished
and partly in the rough, in which the tales were
arranged in groups but not as a whole series;[3] and
editors ever since have laboured to catch his intentions.

What would modern editors give for the opportunity
Chaucer's executors had! Lacking it, they have done
their best to arrange the groups, and Furnivall's order
has been most favoured. Assuming that the references
to the route of the pilgrims (and to a less extent the
indications of time) can be relied on, and that in those
days of bad roads a leisurely pilgrimage from London
to Canterbury would take four days, he obtains the
following table. The capital letters show the breaks
in the series, and for purposes of reference each group of
linked tales is known by the capital that precedes it :—

---

[1] The incomplete Cook's Tale follows the Reeve's on the first day.
But on the last day the Host calls on him as if he had not yet told
a tale. He is then too drunk to respond and the Manciple takes his
place.

[2] But the Monk's Tale is of the kind that might begin or end
anywhere.

[3] This does not imply that at Chaucer's death there was but one
copy of each tale or group. It is probable that some of the tales had
been circulated during his lifetime.

The Pilgrims' Way to Canterbury.

In this arrangement several points are debatable, but at least it is certain that the Nun's Priest's Tale is told not far from Rochester (because when the Host asks the Monk to begin the tale which precedes it he says 'Lo! Rouchestre stant heer faste by!'); that Chaucer thinks of the story as being told on a spring day (he dates the Man of Law's Tale on the 18th of April); and that from the Shipman's Tale [1] to the Nun's Priest's Tale the series is unbroken, with all the links complete.

Such a series enables us to study Chaucer's skill in the management of his materials. In assigning tales to their tellers he observes one general rule: although

---

[1] The linking of the Shipman's Tale with the Man of Law's depends on one MS. of inferior authority; but it is a happy guess.

the pilgrims are nearly all of the middle class,[1] he
more than once distinguishes the 'gentils' from the
rest,[2] and he is careful to give the 'gentils'—the
Knight, Squire, Franklin, Doctor, Man of Law, Monk,
Prioress, Clerk, Parson—tales that conform to courtesy
and 'gentilesse'. As for the order of telling, the
Knight, who is the chief man present, very appro-
priately draws the lot for the first tale, and the Parson
tells the last because all the company are agreed 'to
enden in som vertuous sentence'. But in between
there is no order of precedence. Sometimes the pilgrims take charge, as on the first day when the drunken
Miller follows the Knight because nobody can stop
him, and the Reeve, whom he provokes, is allowed to
tell a tale of a miller in reply. At other times, the
Host, who is the agreed arbiter, calls upon a pilgrim,
reminding him of his compact to obey; and it so
happens that in this particular series the Host fixes
the order throughout.

His principle is simple: he likes variety and contrast, and though he can appreciate a sad tale, he
wants a merry one to follow.[3] But let us watch him
at work. The Shipman's Tale, which is merry and not
genteel, wins his approval :

> 'Wel seyd, by *corpus dominus* !' quod our Hoost,
> 'Now longe moote thou saille by the coost,
> Sire gentil maister, gentil maryneer !'

But he immediately singles out the Prioress by way of

---

[1] Knights were reckoned as leaders of the commons. The only poor
labourer is the Plowman, and he could hardly be omitted in the days of
Piers Plowman.

[2] e. g. in the link following the Knight's Tale and in that before the
Pardoner's Prologue.

[3] After the Doctor's story of Appius and Virginia he declares :
> 'By corpus bones ! but I have triacle,
> Or elles a draughte of moyste and corny ale,
> *Or but I heere anon a myrie tale,*
> Myn herte is lost for pitee of this mayde.'

contrast, and with studied diffidence and courtesy invites her to begin. The Prioress, as might be expected, chooses a religious subject—the exquisite legend of the schoolboy martyr whose heart was set upon singing *O Alma Redemptoris Mater*. When she had finished, says Chaucer,

> every man
> As sobre was that wonder was to se,
> Til that oure Hoostè japen tho began,
> And thanne at erst he looked upon me
> And seydè thus: 'What man artow?' quod he.
> 'Thou lookest as thou woldest fynde an hare,
> For evere upon the ground I se thee stare.[1]
> Approchè neer and looke up murily.
> Now war yow, sires, and lat this man have place;
> He in the waast is shape as wel as I . . .
> He semeth elvyssh[2] by his contenaunce,
> For unto no wight dooth he daliaunce . . .
> *Telle us a tale of myrthe*, and that anon.

Then Chaucer begins 'a rym I lerned longe agoon' —the *Tale of Sir Thopas*, which is the type of rimed romances in their last degeneracy, rich in jingling rimes, elaborate conventional descriptions, elf-queens and three-headed giants, but almost without action. As he begins the second fit. the parody becomes more obvious; and the Host, who had expected 'som deyntee thyng', can bear it no longer:

> 'Namoore of this, for Goddes dignitee!'
> Quod oure Hoostè, 'for thou makest me
> So wery of thy verray lewednesse[3] . . .
> Mine eres aken of thy drasty speche.'

Chaucer asks why he alone should be stopped, since

[1] A critic (*Mod. Lang. Notes*, 1925, p. 54) has urged that this is not a 'permanent' description of Chaucer, and that his eyes were cast down in sadness after the Prioress's tale. But *ever* cannot mean 'for the last ten minutes' (the sad part of the Prioress's tale would take no longer to tell). Besides, something distinctive attracts the Host's attention to Chaucer, and an attitude accounted for by a momentary sadness which all the company share, would not be remarkable.

[2] *elvish* here perhaps means 'moon-struck'.   [3] i. e. rusticity.

it is the best rime he knows, and gets a downright answer :

> 'Thou doost noght elles but despendest tyme,—
> Sire, at o word, thou shalt no lenger ryme.
> Lat se wher thou kanst tellen aught in geeste,[1]
> Or telle in prosé somwhat, at the leeste,
> In which ther be som murthe or som doctrýne.

Chaucer on Pilgrimage. From the Ellesmere MS.

This last suggestion is taken up in Chaucer's tale of Melibeus, which reports the proverbial consolations Dame Prudence gave to her husband Melibeus, after

---

[1] Alliterative verse.

she had been beaten and her daughter wounded to
death by his enemies. It is a testimony to the medieval
liking for didactic works that this story, so wearisome
now, was heard to the end. The Host merely regrets
that his own shrewish wife had not the chance of
hearing it and acquiring a little of the saintly patience
of Dame Prudence. Then he calls on the Monk with
some rough banter, and the too ready response might
have been a warning : 'I shall do my best', says the
Monk,

> 'to tellè yow a tale or two or three,
> And if yow list to herkne hyderward[1]
> I wol yow seyn the lyf of Seint Edward ;
> Or elles first tragédies wol I telle,
> Of whiche I have an hundred in my celle.'

Tragedy it is—the fall of the prosperous—and he
settles down to do it thoroughly, beginning his examples
as far back as Lucifer and Adam. It was a favourite
theme in the Middle Ages, but a monotonous and
gloomy theme for such an occasion ; and when the
Monk reaches his seventeenth tragedy, the Knight,
oppressed perhaps by the thought of the other eighty-
three in his cell, calls ' Hoo ! ' and explains (for he is
a master of tact) that this cumulation of misfortune is
painful to him. The Host avows more bluntly that
he is bored :

> ' Swich talkying is nat worth a boterflye,
> For therinne is ther no desport ne game.'

He longs more than ever for a merry tale, and as the
Monk refuses to tell a hunting story, he calls the Nun's
Priest into the centre of the group of riders : ' Telle
us swich thyng as may oure hertes glade '. This time
he gets the merry tale of the Cock and the Fox.

Modern criticism has gained so much by the close

---

[1] i.e. to me.

study of the frame into which the Canterbury tales
are fitted, that there is a tendency to push ingenuity
in this direction beyond the limits of good sense,
and to interpret the tales themselves as if they were
speeches by the actors in a play. The stressing of
some favourable passages has given rise to the con-
ception of Chaucer as a dramatic genius, which seems
to be radically unsound if 'dramatic' is used in con-
tradistinction to 'narrative', or indeed in any strict
sense. A general congruence there is between his
characters and their words,[1] and he can both devise
appropriate action and describe it ; but these qualities
belong to good narrative as well as to drama. On the
other hand, the detachment of the tales from their
frame is generally well marked : once a tale begins,
it is exceptional to find any certain reference to the
teller, the company, or the pilgrimage, until it ends.[2]
And there are several discordant indications : the
Knight speaks as if he were writing his tale ;[3] so does
the Franklin ;[4] the Canon's Yeoman[5] apologizes to
'Canons religious', though there is none among the
pilgrims, explaining that

> 'This tale was nat oonly toold for yow—
> But eek for othere moo ; '

and in the Merchant's tale, of which the scene is laid
in Italy, Justin, giving advice to his brother on marriage,
refers to the Wife of Bath, Chaucer's own creation![6]

[1] I pass over the Second Nun's Tale (see p. xxxiii, footnote) and the
Shipman's Tale, which was written originally for a woman—probably
the Wife of Bath—assuming that Chaucer would have removed the
anomalies. But a dramatist would scarcely hope to get a good result
by such adaptation.
[2] Where there are special preambles—the Pardoner, Wife of Bath,
Canon's Yeoman—the frame and tale are fused together.
[3] 'But of that storie list me nat to write,' A. 1201.
[4] F. 1548 ff.
[5] Canon's Yeoman's Tale, G. 1000 f. See also the note to ll. 559 ff.
[6] E. 1685 ff. I do not overlook the interpretation of these lines as an

But all of these are explained if Chaucer felt himself
as the teller.[1]   And is not that the impression of most
readers?   Except at the beginning and end, do we
feel in the tale of the Cock and the Fox that it is
a priest who is speaking, and would our enjoyment be
less or different if the tale had been given to the Squire
or the Franklin?   Is the discussion of predestination
(ll. 468 ff.) better suited to a priest in the presence of
his superior, the Prioress, than to the author of *Troilus*
iv. 960 ff.?   Or are the words 'O Gaufred deere
maister soverayn' (l. 581) as apt in the Priest's mouth as
in Chaucer's?   If *The Canterbury Tales* is to be judged
as a drama, it comes off poorly.   The author is an actor
himself, the only one with a doubled part ; he makes the
Man of Law give an account of his earlier poems ;   he
is constantly intruding his own opinions, and peeping
round the curtain to show himself to the audience or see
how they like his work—a serious fault in a dramatist.
But this refusal to be impersonal, and to lose himself
in the creatures of his imagination, has a large part in
Chaucer's greatness as a narrative poet.   He estab-
lishes with his readers a relation so direct, easy, and
personal that his inconsistencies are forgiven ; and no
later poet can rival him in this, for he learned his art
in a school which trained an author to address a group
no larger than the reach of his voice, or a few friends
in his chamber, where he could feel his hold on the
listeners, and respond to every flicker on their faces.

aside by the Merchant, but prefer the reading which has the best manuscript support, and the plain meaning of the words.

[1] He refers to the Wife of Bath in almost the same words in his
Envoy to Bukton 'touching marriage'.

GEOFFREY CHAUCER, son of John Chaucer, wine merchant, of London, was born about 1340. By 1357 he had begun his career as a page in the household of Lionel, Duke of Clarence. In 1359 he was with the army in France: he was taken prisoner, and his ransom was paid in March 1360. In 1367 he received a pension as a member (*dilectus valettus*) of the King's household. In 1369, on the death of Blanche, wife of John of Gaunt, he wrote his *Deth of Blanche the Duchesse*, the first evidence of an important friendship with John of Gaunt.

He became a trusted member of the diplomatic service, visiting France several times (1369–78), Flanders (1377), Italy (1372–3 and 1378); and he was successful, if we may judge from the favours that came his way:—another pension, a pitcher of wine daily, the Comptrollership of the Customs of Wools, Skins, and Hides (1374); the wardship of two minors (1375); the proceeds of a heavy fine (1376); the sinecure Comptrollership of Petty Customs at London (1382); and the right to discharge his other more onerous Comptrollership by deputy (1385). In 1386 he became member of Parliament for Kent. During this prosperous period he wrote his version of *Boethius*; the *Hous of Fame*; the *Parlement of Foules* (1382?); *Troilus*; and the *Legend of Good Women* (1386?); and he probably planned the *Canterbury Tales*, his last great work.

But with the failure of John of Gaunt's party in the autumn of 1386, he lost both his Comptrollerships: and he saw lean days till 1389, when Richard II made him Commissioner of Works. This post, too, he lost in 1391: but in 1394 another pension was granted him. In his latter years he was often in debt. We need not picture him in misery, for debt is sometimes the result of living well. In 1399 he greeted the new king Henry IV with his last work, the *Compleynt to his Purse*. It gained him another pension, which he did not long enjoy. He died in 1400, and was buried in Westminster Abbey.

He had married Philippa, a lady of the court, perhaps in 1366. She died in 1387. For a 'litel son Lowis', then ten years old and at Oxford, he wrote the *Treatise on the Astrolabe* in 1391.

THE TEXT

THE text is based on the published facsimile of the Ellesmere MS., with reference to the Chaucer Society's prints of seven other complete MSS. of the Tales, and particularly to the Hengwrt and Corpus MSS.

In this tale the Ellesmere text is generally careful, but it has several patent errors (e.g. ll. 128, 161, 165, 448, 496, 526, 596, 656), and none of its peculiar readings is so good that it can be retained with certainty. Hengwrt, because of its near relation to Ellesmere, is a valuable check on arbitrary scribal changes in that MS.; but in the Nun's Priest's Tale its contamination with the Corpus group (e.g. in the omission of ll. 5-24) lessens its value as a witness to the original of the Ellesmere text. The Corpus MS., though careless in general, has some readings of independent authority, and I have assumed that in one place at least, l. 620, it enables us to get behind an error common to the other groups of MSS. (see the note). In this line the reading of the Harleian MS. 7334, which has been accepted by most modern editors, should be rejected. In the Nun's Priest's Tale the Harleian MS. has many readings in common with the Corpus type; it contributes nothing of value to the text; and even if *y-gon* in l. 652 is right, it is better explained as an obvious emendation by the editor of the Harleian text than as an original reading preserved only in that branch of the MS. tradition.

The acceptance of the Epilogue (see note to l. 43), or any part of it, as Chaucer's work raises difficult problems, for it is not in the best MSS.—of the eight printed by the Chaucer Society only Cambridge Dd. contains it. We need to know how it got into the inferior MSS., or how it got out of the majority and the best, and no really satisfactory explanation has been put forward. To assume that Chaucer left one manuscript which contained in the form of marginalia, interlineations, &c. all the variant readings it is convenient to attribute to him, is an elaborate way of evading the problems set by divergences in the extant MSS.

Every departure from the Ellesmere MS. is recorded in the footnotes, where *MS.* indicates that the reading is found only in Ellesmere, and *MS. &c.* that at least one of the printed manuscripts agrees with Ellesmere. Some noteworthy variants taken from the prints of the other MSS. are also included. In choosing these, regard has been had to the most authoritative classifications of the MSS.; but it seemed better not to specify the sources of the variants, as the information would necessarily be incomplete and misleading. The verse paragraphs of the Ellesmere MS. are preserved. Capitals, punctuation, and the use of *v : u, j : i* are modern. Where final -*e* must be pronounced as a separate syllable to make up the rhythm, I have printed *ė*, except at the end of the line, where -*e* is normally syllabic, and in words like *nevere* (pronounced *nev/re*) where *never* would serve for the metre. Divergences from the modern English incidence of stress are marked by accents placed over the first vowel of the stressed syllable : an acute accent when the first or second syllable is stressed, e. g. *tragédie* ; a grave accent where the third, fourth, or fifth syllable is stressed, e. g. *ascencìòun*, *altercacìòun*. This method has the advantage of showing that *ascencìòun* must be read as *a/scen/ci/oun*, with four syllables, and *Pharaò* as *Pha/ra/o* with three. The first syllable of a nine-syllable line is also marked with the acute accent.

MATERIALS FOR THE TEXT

The Ellesmere Chaucer reproduced in facsimile, 2 vols, Manchester 1911.

Chaucer Society's Publications, Series I, especially

   The Six-Text Chaucer (1868–).

   The separate prints of *MS. Harley 7334* (1885) and *MS. Cambridge Univ. Dd. 4. 24* (1901-2).

Skeat, W. W. *The Works of Geoffrey Chaucer*, 7 vols., Oxford 1894-7.

Koch. J. *A Detailed Comparison of the Eight MSS. of the Canterbury Tales* &c., Heidelberg 1913.

SELECT BIBLIOGRAPHY [1]

BIBLIOGRAPHICAL.

Hammond, Miss E. P., *Chaucer : A Bibliographical Manual*, New York 1908. [Excellent.]

Wells, J. E., *A Manual of the Writings in Middle English, 1050–1400*, New Haven &c. 1916; Supplements, 1919, 1924.

Brusendorff, A., *The Chaucer Tradition*, London 1925. [Stimulating, but uneven.]

Petersen, Miss K. O., *On the Sources of the Nonnè Prestes Tale*, Boston 1898. [Good detailed study.]

COMPLETE EDITIONS (in one volume).

Skeat, W. W., *The Student's Chaucer*, Oxford 1895.

Pollard, A. W. (and others), *The Works of Geoffrey Chaucer*, Globe edition, London 1903.

STUDIES OF THE PERIOD.

Jusserand, J. J., *English Wayfaring Life in the Middle Ages*, (transl. L. Toulmin Smith), London 1899; revised 1921.

Oman, C., *The Great Revolt of 1381*, Oxford 1906.

Trevelyan, G. M., *England in the Age of Wycliffe*, London 1899; new edn. 1909.

CHAUCER'S PREDECESSORS.

Ker, W. P., *English Literature, Medieval*, London 1912.

Sisam, K., and Tolkien, J. R. R., *Fourteenth Century Verse and Prose*, Oxford 1921, &c.

CRITICAL STUDIES OF CHAUCER.

Dryden, John, Preface to his *Fables*, 1700. [The Nun's Priest's Tale is the second Fable.]

Kittredge, G. L., *Chaucer and his Poetry*, Cambridge (U.S.A.) and London 1915.

Legouis, E., *Chaucer* (transl. L. Lailavoix), London 1913.

Pollard, A. W., *A Primer of Chaucer*, London 1893, &c.

---

[1] The bibliographical manuals cited give a full account of the great body of Chaucer criticism contained in special editions, monographs, and journals. As I have found it impossible to give specific references to such sources, I take this opportunity of making a general acknowledgement.

END OF THE MONK'S TALE

lines 737–76.

This richè Cresus, whilom kyng of Lyde,
Of whichè Cresus Cirus soore hym dradde,
Yet was he caught amyddes al his pryde,
And to be brent men to the fyr hym ladde ;   740
But swich a reyn doun fro the welkne shadde
That slow the fyr and made hym to escape ;
But to be war no gracè yet he hadde,
Til Fortune on the galwes made hym gape.

Whanne he escaped was, he kan nat stente   745
For to bigynne a newè werre agayn ;
He wendè wel, for that Fortúne hym sente
Swich hap that he escaped thurgh the rayn,
That of hise foos he myghtè nat be slayn ;
And eek a swevene upon a nyght he mette   750
Of which he was so proud and eek so fayn
That in vengeánce he al his hertè sette.

Upon a tree he was, as that hym thoughte,
Ther Juppiter hym wessh bothe bak and syde,
And Phebus eek a fair towáille hym broughte,   755
To drye hym with; and therfore wax his pryde,
And to his doghter that stood hym bisyde,
Which that he knew in heigh sciénce habounde,
He bad hire telle hym what it signyfyde,
And she his dreem bigan right thus expounde :   760

' The tree,' quod she, ' the galwes is to meene,
And Juppiter bitokneth snow and reyn,
And Phebus with his towaillè so clene—
Tho been the sonnè stremes for to seyn.
Thou shalt anhanged be, fader, certéyn :   765
Reyn shal thee wasshe, and sonnè shal thee drye.'
Thus warned hym ful plat and ful pleyn
His doghter, which that called was Phanýe.

Anhanged was Cresus the proudè kyng,
His roial tronè myghte hym nat availle.   770
Tragedie is noon oother maner thyng,
Ne kan in syngyng crie ne biwaille,
Bút that Fortune alwey wole assaille
With unwar strook the regnes that been proude ;
For whan men trusteth hire, thanne wol she faille   775
And covere hire brightè facè with a clowde.

Explicit Tragedia.

Heere stynteth the Knyght the Monk of his tale.

The Prologe of the NONNES PREESTES TALE.

'HOO!' quod the Knyght, 'good sire, namoore
    of this!
That ye han seyd is right ynough, ywis,
And muchel moore ; for litel hevynesse
Is right ynough to muchė folk, I gesse.   (B 3960)
I seye for me, it is a greet disese,   5
Where as men han been in greet welthe and ese,
To heeren of hire sodeyn fal, allas!
And the contrárie is joye and greet solás,
As whan a man hath been in povre estaat,
And clymbeth up, and wexeth fortunat,   10
And there abideth in prosperitee :
Swich thyng is gladsom, as it thynketh me,
And of swich thyng were goodly for to telle.'
  'Ye,' quod oure Hoost, ' by seintė Poules belle!
Ye seye right sooth.   This Monk he clappeth lowde :
He spak, how "Fortune covered with a clowde"— 16
I noot nevere what—and also of a "Tragédie"
(Right now ye herde), and pardee, no remédie
It is for to biwaillė ne compleyne
That that is doon ; and als it is a peyne,   20
As ye han seyd, to heere of hevynesse.

1 of *om. MS.*   5–24 *om. some MSS.*   14 seint *MS.* &c.

Sire Monk, namoore of this, so God yow blesse!
Youre tale anoyeth al this compaignye:
Swich talkyng is nat worth a boterflye,   (B 3980)
For therinne is ther no desport ne game.   25
    Wherfore sire Monk, daun Piers by youre name,
I pray yow hertėly, telle us somwhat elles,
For sikerly, nere clynkyng of youre belles
That on youre bridel hange on every syde,
By hevene-kyng that for us allė dyde!   30
I sholde er this han fallen doun for sleep,
Althogh the slough had never been so deep;
Thanne haddė youre tale al be toold in veyn:
For, certeinly, as that thise clerkes seyn,
Where as a man may have noon audiènce,   35
Noght helpeth it to tellen his senténce.
And wel I woot the substance is in me,
If any thyng shal wel reported be:
Sire, sey somwhat of huntyng, I yow preye.'
    'Nay,' quod this Monk, 'I have no lust to pleye; 40
Now lat another telle, as I have toold.'
    Thanne spak oure Hoost, with rudė speche and boold,
And seyde unto the Nonnes Preest anon,   (B 3999)
'Com neer, thou preest, com hyder thou, sir John;
Telle us swich thyng as may oure hertes glade;   45
Be blithė, though thou ryde upon a jade;
What thogh thyn hors be bothė foul and lene?
If he wol serve thee, rekkė nat a bene!
Looke that thyn herte be murie everemo.'
    'Yis sire,' quod he, 'yis, Hoost, so moot I go!   50
But I be myrie, ywis I wol be blamed.'
And right anon his tale he hath attamed,
And thus he seyde unto us everichon,
This sweetė preest, this goodly man, sir John.

Explicit.

25 *MSS. which omit ll.* 5–24 *have* Youre talcs doon us no &c.

Heere bigynneth

THE NONNES PREESTES TALE

OF THE COK AND HEN, CHAUNTECLEER AND
PERTELOTE.

A POVRE wydwė, somdeel stape in age,   55
   Was whilom dwellyng in a narwe cotáge
Biside a grevė, stondynge in a dale.
This wydwe, of which I tellė yow my tale,
Syn thilkė day that she was last a wyf,
In paciènce ladde a ful symple lyf,   60
For litel was hir catel and hir rente :
By housbondrie of swich as God hire sente
She foond hirself and eek hir doghtren two.
Thre largė sowes haddė she and namo,   (B 4020)
Thre keen, and eek a sheep that hightė Malle   65
Ful sooty was hir bour and eek hir halle,
In which she eet ful many a sklendre meel :
Of poynaunt sauce hir neded never a deel ;
No deyntee morsel passed thurgh hir throte,
Hir diete was accordant to hir cote ;   70
Repleccioun ne made hire nevere sik,

excess

Attempree diete was al hir phisik,
And exercise, and hertes súffisàunce.
The goutè lette hire nothyng for to daunce
N'apoplexiè shentè nat hir heed.   75
No wyn ne drank she, neither whit ne reed,
Hir bord was served moost with whit and blak,—
Milk and broun breed, in which she foond no lak,—
Seynd bacoun, and somtyme an ey or tweye,
For she was, as it were, a maner deye.   80
   A yeerd she hadde, enclosed al aboute
With stikkes and a dryè dych withoute,
In which she hadde a Cok heet Chauntècleer:
In al the land of crowyng nas his peer ;   (B 4040)
His voys was murier than the murie orgón   85
On messèdayes that in the chirchè gon ;
Wel sikerer was his crowyng in his logge
Than is a clokke, or any abbéy orlogge :
By nature he knew ech ascenciòun
Of the equynoxiàl in thilkè toun,   90
For whan degrees fiftenè were ascended,
Thanne crew he, that it myghte nat been amended.
His coomb was redder than the fyn corál,
And batailled as it were a castel wal ;
His byle was blak and as the jeet it shoon,   95
Lyk asure were hise legges and his toon,
Hise nayles whitter than the lylye flour,
And lyk the burned gold was his colóur.
This gentil cok hadde in his governàunce
Sevene hennes, for to doon al his plesáunce,   100
Whiche were hise sustres and his paramours,
And wonder lyk to hym as of colóurs ;
Of whiche the faireste hewed on hir throte
Was cleped fairè damoysele Pertèlote.   (B 4060)

75 N'apoplexiè] Ne poplexie ne *some MSS.*   83 heet] highte ; that
highte *some MSS.*   88 any] an *MS.* &c.   89 knew] crew *MS.*
90 the *omitted in some MSS.*   91 weren *MS.*

Curteys she was, discreet and debonaire,   105
And cómpaignàble, and bar hyrself so faire
Syn thilkè day that she was seven-nyght oold,
That trewèly she hath the herte in hoold
Of Chauntècleer, loken in every lith :   *link*
He loved hire so that wel was hym therwith.   110
And swich a joye was it to here hem synge,
Whan that the brightè sonnè gan to sprynge,
In sweete accord, ' My lief is faren in londe ':   *far away*
For thilkè tyme, as I have understonde,
Beestes and briddes koudè speke and synge.   115

  And so bifel that in a dawènynge,
As Chauntècleer among hise wyves alle
Sat on his perchè, that was in the halle,
And next hym sat this fairè Pertèlote,
This Chauntècleer gan gronen in his throte,   120
As man that in his dreem is drecched soore.   *distressed*

  And whan that Pertèlote thus herde hym roore,
She was agast, and seydè, ' Hertè deere,
What eyleth yow, to grone in this manére?   (B 4080)
Ye been a verray slepere, fy, for shame ! '   125

  And he answérde and seydè thus, ' Madáme,
I pray yow that ye take it nat agrief :
By God, me mette I was in swich meschíef
Right now, that yet myn herte is soore afright.
Now God,' quod he, ' my swevene recche aright,   130 *interpret*
And kepe my body out of foul prisóun !
Me mette how that I romed up and doun
Withinne oure yeerd, wheer as I saugh a beest
Was lyk an hound, and wolde han maad areest
Upon my body and han had me deed.   135
His colour was bitwixè yelow and reed,
And tipped was his tayl and bothe hise eeris

112 gan] bigan *MS.* &c.   116 a] the *MS.*   123 O herte *MS.*
128 mette] thoughte *MS.*   130 recche] rede *some MSS.*   135 han]
wolde han *some MSS.*

With blak, unlyk the remenant of hise heeris ;
His snowtè smal, with glowynge eyen tweye—
Yet of his look for feere almoost I deye !   140
This caused me my gronyng, doutèlees.'
    'Avoy !' quod she, ' Fy on yow, hertèlees !
Allas,' quod she, ' for, by that God above !
Now han ye lost myn herte and al my love.   (B 4100)
I kan nat love a coward, by my feith !   145
For certes, whatso any womman seith,
We alle desiren, if it myghtè bee,
To han housbondes hardy, wise and free,
And secree, and no nygard, ne no fool,
Ne hym that is agast of every tool,   150   *weapon*
Ne noon avauntour :—by that God above !
How dorste ye seyn, for shame, unto youre love
That any thyng myghte makè yow aferd ?
Have ye no mannes herte, and han a berd ?
    Allas ! and konne ye been agast of swevenys ?   155
Nothyng, God woot ! but vanitee in swevene is.
Swevenes engendren of replecciòuns,
And ofte of fume and of complecciòuns,   *vapours*
Whan humours been to habundant in a wight.
    Certes this dreem which ye han met tonyght   160
Comth of the gretè superfluytee
Óf youre redè colera, pardee,
Which causeth folk to dreden in hir dremes
Of arwes, and of fyr with redè lemes ;   (B 4120)   *flame*
Of redè beestes, that they wol hem byte ;   165
Of conteks, and of whelpes grete and lyte ;
Right as the humour of maléncolìe
Causeth ful many a man in sleep to crie
For feere of blakè beres, or boles blake,
Or elles blakè develes wol hem take.   170

161 comth] cometh *MS.* &c. : the grete] greet *MS.*   163 dreden]
dremen *some MSS.*   165 rede] grete *MS.*   169 of beres and of
boles blake *some MSS.*

Of othere humours koude I telle also
That werken many a man in sleep ful wo,
But I wol passe as lightly as I kan.

    Lo Catoun, which that was so wys a man,
Seyde he nat thus, " ne do no fors ef dremes"?   175
    Now, sire,' quod she, ' whan we flee fro the bemes,
For goddes love, as taak som laxatyf!
Up peril of my soule and of my lyf,
I conseille yow the beste (I wol nat lye)
That bothe of colere and of maléncolÿe   180
Ye purgė yow ; and for ye shal nat tarie,
Though in this toun is noon apothecarie,
I shal myself to herbes techen yow   (B 4139)
That shul been for youre heele and for youre prow :
And in oure yeerd tho herbes shal I fynde   185
The whiche han of hire propreteė by kynde
To purgė yow, bynethe and eek above.
Foryet nat this, for Goddes owene love !
Ye been ful coleryk of complecciòun :
Warė the sonne in his ascenciòun   190
Ne fynde yow nat repleet of humours hoote.
And if it do, I dar wel leye a grote
That ye shul have a fevere terciàne,
Ór an agu that may be youre bane.
A day or two ye shul have digestyves   195
Of wormes, er ye take youre laxatyves
Of lawriol, centáure, and fumetère,
Or elles of ellèbor that groweth there,
Of katapucė, or of gaitrys beryis,
Of herbe-yve growyng in oure yeerd ther mery is.   200
Pekke hem up right as they growe, and ete hem yn !
Be myrie, housbonde, for youre fader kyn !
Dredeth no dreem,—I kan sey yow namoore.'   (B 4159)
    ' Madame,' quod he, ' graunt mercy of youre loore.

But nathélees, as touchyng daun Catóun   205
That hath of wysdom swich a greet renoun,
Though that he bad no dremes for to drede,
By God! men may in oldé bookes rede
Of many a man moore of auctorité
Than evere Caton was, so moot I thee!   210
That al the révers seyn of his senténce,
And han wel founden by experience
That dremes been significaciòuns
As wel of joye as of tribulaciòuns
That folk enduren in this lif présent.   215
Ther nedeth make of this noon argument:
The verray preevè sheweth it in dede.

Oon of the gretteste auctour that mén rede
Seith thus: that whilom two feláwes wente
On pilgrimage in a ful good entente,   220
And happed so they coomen in a toun,
Wher as ther was swich congregaciòun
Of peple, and eek so streit of herbergage,
That they ne founde as muche as o cotáge   (B 4180)
In which they bothè myghte y-logged bee;   225
Wherfore they mosten, of necessitee,
As for that nyght departen compaignye,
And ech of hem gooth to his hostelrye,
And took his loggyng as it woldè falle:
That oon of hem was logged in a stalle,   230
Fer in a yeerd, with oxen of the plough;
That oother man was logged wel ynough,
As was his áventùre or his fortúne,
That us govérneth alle as in commúne.

And so bifel that, longe er it were day,   235
This man mette in his bed, ther as he lay,
How that his felawe gan upon hym calle,
And seyde, "Allas, for in an oxes stalle

211 his] this *MS.*   212 And] That *MS.*   225 y-logged]
logged *MS.*

This nyght I shal be mordred ther I lye!
Now help me, deerė brother, or I dye!   240
In allė hastė com to me!" he sayde.

   This man out of his sleep for feere abrayde,
But whan that he was wakened of his sleep,
He turned hym and took of this no keep: (B 4200)
Hym thoughte his dreem nas but a vanitee.   245
Thus twies in his slepyng dremed hee,
And attė thriddė tyme yet his feláwe
Cam, as hym thoughte, and seide. "I am now slawe:
Bihoold my bloody woundes, depe and wyde!
Arys up erly in the morwė-tyde,   250
And at the westgate of the toun," quod he,
"A cartė ful of donge ther shaltow se,
In which my body is hid ful privėly:
Do thilkė carte arresten boldėly.
My gold caused my mordre, sooth to sayn"—   255
And tolde hym every point how he was slayn,
With a ful pitous facė, pale of hewe.
And trustė wel, his dreem he foond ful trewe;
For on the morwe, as soone as it was day,
To his feláwes in he took the way,   260
And whan that he cam to this oxes stalle,
After his felawe he bigan to calle.

   The hostiler answėrede hym anon,
And seydė, "Sire, youre felawe is agon;   (B 4220)
As soone as day he wente out of the toun."   265

   This man gan fallen in suspeciòun,
Remembrynge on hise dremes that he mette,
And forth he gooth—no lenger wolde he lette—
Unto the westgate of the toun, and fond
A dong-carte, as it were to dongė lond,   270
That was arrayed in that samė wise
As ye han herd the dedė man devyse;

244 this] it *MS*.   263 answerde *MS*. &c.   266 falle in gret s.
some MSS.   270 wente as it were *some MSS*; as he wente *others*.

And with an hardy herte he gan to crye :
Vengeance and justice of this felonye :
" My felawe mordred is this same nyght,   275
And in this carte heere he lith gapyng upright !
I crye out on the ministres," quod he,
" That sholden kepe and reulen this citée !
Harrow ! allas ! heere lith my felawe slayn ! "
What sholde I moore unto this talé sayn ?   280
The peple out-sterte and caste the cart to grounde,
And in the myddel of the dong they founde
The dede man, that mordred was al newe.

   O blisful God, that art so just and trewe,   (B 4240)
Lo, how that thou biwreyest mordre alway !   285
Mordre wol out, that se we day by day.
Mordre is so wlatsom and abhomynable
To God, that is so just and resonable,
That he ne wol nat suffre it heled be,   *conceal*
Though it abyde a yeer, or two, or thre :   290
Mordre wol out, this my conclusioun.
And right anon ministres of that toun
Han hent the cartere and so soore hym pyned,
And eek the hostiler so soore engyned,
That they biknewe hire wikkednesse anon,   295
And were anhanged by the nekke-bon.

   Heere may men seen that dremes been to drede !
And certes, in the same book I rede,
Right in the nexte chapitre after this
(I gabbe nat, so have I joye or blis !) :—   300

   Two men that wolde han passed over see,
For certeyn cause, into a fer contrée,
If that the wynd ne hadde been contrárie,
That made hem in a citee for to tarie   (B 4260)
That stood ful myrie upon an haven-syde :   305
But on a day, agayn the even-tyde,

The wynd gan chaunge and blew right as hem leste.
Jolif and glad they wente unto hir reste,
And casten hem ful erly for to saille.

But (herkneth!) to that o man fil a greet mervaille.
That oon of hem, in slepyng as he lay,   311
Hym mette a wonder dreem, agayn the day :—
Hym thoughte a man stood by his beddes syde
And hym comanded that he sholde abyde,
And seyde hym thus, " If thou tomorwe wende,   315
Thow shalt be dreynt—my tale is at an ende."

He wook and tolde his felawe what he mette,
And preyede hym his viagé to lette,—
As for that day he preyede hym to byde.

His felawe, that lay by his beddes syde,   320
Gan for to laughe and scorned hym ful faste.
" No dreem," quod he, " may so myn herte agaste
That I wol letté for to do my thynges.
I setté nat a straw by thy dremynges,   (B 4280)
For swevenes been but vanytees and japes :   325
Men dreme alday of owles or of apes,
And of many a mazé therwithal ;
Men dreme of thyng that nevere was, ne shal.
But sith I see that thou wolt heere abyde,
And thus forslewthen wilfully thy tyde,   330
God woot, it reweth me, and have good day."
And thus he took his leve and wente his way.
But er that he hadde half his cours y-seyled,
Noot I nat why, ne what myschaunce it eyled,
But casuelly the shippes botme rente,   335
And ship and man under the water wente,
In sighte of othere shippes it bisyde
That with hem seyled at the samé tyde.
And therfore, fairé Pertélote so deere,

---

308 wenten unto reste *some MSS.*   318 preyde *MS.* &c : for to
lette *some MSS.*   319 preyde *MS.* &c.   338 hem] hym *some MSS.*

By swiche ensamples oldè maistow leere   340
That no man sholdè been to recchèlees
Of dremes, for I seye thee, doutèlees,
That many a dreem ful soore is for to drede.

Lo, in the lyf of Seint Kenelm I rede,   (B 4300)
That was Kenulphus sone, the noble kyng   345
Of Mercenrike, how Kenelm mette a thyng.
A lite er he was mordred, on a day,
His mordre in his avysìoun he say.
His norice hym expowned every deel
His swevene, and bad hym for to kepe hym weel 350
For traisoun ; but he nas but seven yeer oold,
And therfore litel talè hath he toold
Of any dreem, so hooly was his herte.
By God ! I haddè levere than my sherte
That ye hadde rad his legende, as have I.   355
Dame Pertèlote, I sey you trewèly,
Macrobeus, that writ the Avisìoun
In Affrike of the worthy Cipìoun,
Affermeth dremes, and seith that they been
Warnynge of thynges that men after seen.   360
    And forthermoore, I pray yow, looketh wel
In the Oldè Testament of Danièl,
If he heeld dremes any vanitee.

Reed eek of Joseph, and ther shul ye see   (B 4320)
Wher dremes be somtyme (I sey nat alle)   365
Warnynge of thynges that shul after falle.

Looke of Egipte the kyng, daun Pharaò,
His bakere and his butiller also,
Wher they ne feltè noon effect in dremes !
Whoso wol seken actes of sondry remes   370
May rede of dremes many a wonder thyng :—
    Lo Cresus, which that was of Lydè kyng,
Mette he nat that he sat upon a tree,

340 olde yet *MS.*   346 Mertenrike *MS.* &c.   353 was] is *MS.*

Which signified he sholde anhanged bee?

   Lo heere Andromacha, Ectóres wyf,   375
That day that Ector sholdė lese his lyf
She dremed on the samė nyght biforn
How that the lyf of Ector sholde be lorn
If thilkė day he wente into batáille.
She warned hym, but it myghte nat availle: 380
He wentė for to fightė nathéles,
But he was slayn anon of Áchilles.
But thilkė tale is al to longe to telle,
And eek it is ny day,—I may nat dwelle.   (B 4340)
Shortly I seye, as for conclusiòun,   385
That I shal han of this avisiòun
Adversitee; and I seye forthermoor
That I ne telle of laxatyves no stoor,
For they been venymes, I woot it weel;
I hem diffye, I love hem never a deel.   390
   Now lat us speke of myrthe and stynte al this.
Madámė Pertėlote, so have I blis!
Of o thyng God hath sent me largė grace,
For whan I se the beautee of youre face,   (B 4350)
Ye been so scarlet-reed aboute youre eyen,   395
It maketh al my dredė for to dyen.
For, al so siker as *In principio,*
Mulier est hominis confusio:
   Madame, the sentence of this Latyn is,   (B 4355)
"Womman is mannes joye and al his blis.". . .   400
I am so ful of joye and of solás   (B 4360)
That I diffyė bothė swevene and dreem.'   405
And with that word he fly doun fro the beem,
(For it was day) and eke hise hennes alle,
And with a chuk he gan hem for to calle,
For he hadde founde a corn lay in the yerd.
Real he was, he was namoore aferd: . . .   410

375 Adromacha *MS.* &c.   383 tale *om. MS.*: for to telle *MS.*
389 venymous *some MSS.*   406 fly] fleigh; fley *other MSS.*

He looketh as it were a grym leóun,
And on hise toos he rometh up and doun,—
Hym deigned nat to sette his foot to grounde.   415
He chukketh whan he hath a corn y-founde,
And to hym rennen thanne hise wyves alle.
Thus, real as a prince is in his halle,
Leve I this Chauntècleer in his pastúre,
And after wol I telle his áventùre.   420

W̌han that the monthe in which the world bigan,
That hightè March, whan God first maked man,
Wás compleet, and passed were also
(Syn March bigan) thritty dayes and two,   (B 4380)
Bifel that Chauntècleer in al his pryde,   425
Hise sevene wyves walkynge hym bisyde,
Caste up hise eyen to the brightè sonne
That in the signe of Taurus hadde y-ronne
Twenty degrees and oon and somwhat moore,
And knew by kynde, and by noon oother loore,   430
That it was pryme, and crew with blisful stevene.
' The sonne,' he seyde, ' is clomben up on hevene
Fourty degrees and oon and moore, ywis.
Madamè Pertèlote, my worldes blis,
Herkneth thise blisful briddes how they synge,   435
And se the fresshè floures how they sprynge !
Ful is myn herte of revel and solás.'
But sodeynly hym fil a sorweful cas,
For evere the latter ende of joy is wo:
God woot that worldly joye is soone ago!   440
And if a rethor koudè faire endite,
He in a cronycle saufly myghte it write
As for a sovereyn notabilitee.
Now every wys man, lat him herkne me: (B 4400)
This storie is al so trewe, I undertake,   445

418 real] roial *MS.* &c. : his] an *MS.* &c.   426 hym bisyde] by his
syde *MS.*   442 cronique *some MSS.*

As is the book of Launcelot de Lake
That wommen holde in ful greet reverence.
Now wol I torne agayn to my senténce.

    A colfox, ful of sly iniquitee,
That in the grove hadde woned yéres three,   450
By heigh ymaginacióun forncast,
The samé nyght thurghout the hegges brast
Into the yerd ther Chauntécleer the faire
Was wont, and eek hise wyves, to repaire;
And in a bed of wortes stille he lay   455
Til it was passed undren of the day,
Waitynge his tyme on Chauntécleer to falle,—
As gladly doon thise homycides alle
That in await liggen to mordre men.
O falsé mordrour, lurkynge in thy den!   460
O newé Scariot! newé Genyloun!
Falsé dissymulour, O Greek Synóun
That broghtest Troye al outrély to sorwe!
O Chauntécleer, acursed be that morwe   (B 4420)
That thou into that yerd flaugh fro the bemes!   465
Thou were ful wel y-warned by thy dremes
That thilké day was perilous to thee.
But what that God forwoot moot nedes bee,
After the opinióun of certein clerkis;
Witnesse on hym that any parfit clerk is   470
That in scole is greet altercacióun
In this matéere, and greet dispútisòun,
And hath been of an hundred thousand men.
But I ne kan nat bulte it to the bren,
As kan the hooly doctour Agustyn,   475
Or Boece or the Bisshop Bradwardyn :—
Wheither that Goddes worthy forwityng
Streyneth me nedély for to doon a thyng,

448 torne] come *MS.*   465 that (2nd)] the *some MSS.*
478 nedély for] nedefully *MS.*

(Nedély clepe I symple necessitee) ;
Or elles if free choys be graunted me   480
To do that samé thyng or do it noght,
Though God forwoot it er that it was wroght ;
Or if his wityng streyneth never a deel
But by necessitee condicioneel,—   (B 4440)
I wol nat han to do of swich matéere :   485
My tale is of a cok, as ye may heere,
That took his conseil of his wyf with sorwe
To walken in the yerd upon that morwe
That he hadde met the dreem that I yow tolde.
'Wommennes conseils been ful ofté colde ; '   490
Wommannes conseil broghte us first to wo,
And made Adám fro Paradys to go,
Ther as he was ful myrie and wel at ese.
But for I noot to whom it myght displese
If I conséil of wommen woldé blame,   495
Passe over, for I seyde it in my game.
Rede auctours where they trete of swich matéere,
And what they seyn of wommen ye may heere.
Thise been the cokkes wordes and nat myne :
I kan noon harm of no womman divyne.   500

    Faire in the soond to bathe hire myrily
Lith Pertélote, and alle hire sustres by,
Agayn the sonne ; and Chauntécleer so free
Soong murier than the mermayde in the see   (B 4460)
(For Phisiologus seith sikerly   505
How that they syngen wel and myrily).
    And so bifel that as he caste his eye
Among the wortes on a boterflye,
He was war of this fox that lay ful lowe.
Nothyng ne liste hym thanné for to crowe,   510
But cride anon, 'cok ! cok !' and up he sterte,

---

489 the] that *MS.* : yow] of *MS.*   492 fro] out of *MS.*   496 seyde]
seye *MS.*   500 of] on *some MSS.*

As man that was affrayed in his herte;
For natureelly a beest desireth flee
Fro his contrárie, if he may it see,
Though he never erst hadde seyn it with his eye.   515
   This Chauntécleer, whan he gan hym espye,
He wolde han fled, but that the fox anon
Seyde, 'Gentil sire, allas, wher wol ye gon?
Be ye affrayed of me that am youre freend?
Now certes I were worsé than a feend   520
If I to yow wolde harm or vileynye.
I am nat come youre conseil for t'espye,
But trewély the cause of my comynge
Was oonly for to herkne how that ye synge;   (B 4480)
For trewély ye have as myrie a stevene   525
As any aungel hath that is in hevene.
Therwith ye han in musyk moore feelynge
Than hadde Boéce, or any that kan synge.
My lord youre fader (God his soulé blesse!)
And eek youre mooder, of hire gentillesse   530
Han in myn hous y-been, to my greet ese;
And certes, sire, ful fayn wolde I yow plese.
   But for men speke of syngyng, I wol seye,
So moote I brouké wel myne eyen tweye!
Save yow, I herdé nevere man so synge   535
As dide youre fader in the morwénynge.
Certes it was of herte al that he song!
And for to make his voys the mooré strong
He wolde so peyne hym that with bothe hise eyen
He mosté wynke, so loude he woldé cryen,   540
And stonden on his tiptoon therwithal,
And strecché forth his nekké, long and smal
And eek he was of swich discreciòun
That ther nas no man in no regiòun   (B 4500)
That hym in song or wisedom myghté passe.   545

526 hath] *om. MS.*   533 wol] wol yow *MS.*   535 herdé I *MS.*
535 so] yet *MS.*

I have wel rad in daun Burnel the Asse,
Among hise vers, how that ther was a cok,
Fór a preestes sone yaf hym a knok
Upon his leg, whil he was yong and nyce,
He made hym for to lese his benefice.   550
But certeyn ther nys no comparisòun
Bitwixe the wisedom and discreciòun
Óf youre fader, and of his subtiltee.
Now syngeth, sire, for seintè charitee!
Lat se konne ye youre fader countrefete.'   555
    This Chauntècleer hise wynges gan to bete,
As man that koude his traysoun nat espie,
So was he ravysshed with his flaterie.
    (Allas, ye lordes! many a fals flatóur
Is in youre court, and many a losengeour,   560
That plesen yow wel moorè, by my feith,
Than he that soothfastnesse unto yow seith.
Redeth Ecclesiaste of Flaterye;
Beth war, ye lordes, of hir trecherye!)   (B 4520)
    This Chauntècleer stood hye upon his toos,   565
Strecchynge his nekke, and heeld hise eyen cloos,
And gan to crowè loudè for the nones;
And daun Russell the fox stirte up at ones
And by the gargat hentè Chauntècleer,
And on his bak toward the wode hym beer,   570
For yet ne was ther no man that hym sewed.
    O Destinee, that mayst nat been eschewed!
Allas, that Chauntècleer fleigh fro the bemes!
Allas, his wyf ne roghtè nat of dremes!
And on a Friday fil al this meschaunce.   575
    O Venus, that art goddesse of plesáunce,
Syn that thy servant was this Chauntècleer,
And in thy servyce dide al his powéer,
Moore for delit than world to multiplye,
Why woldestow suffre hym on thy day to dye?   580

548 for that *MS*.   560 courtes *MS*.

O Gaufred, deerė maister sovėrayn,
That whan thy worthy kyng Richard was slayn
With shot, compleynedest his deeth so soore,
Why ne hadde I now thy sentence and thy loore
The Friday for to chide, as diden ye?   585
(For on a Friday, soothly, slayn was he).   (B 4542)
Thanne wolde I shewe yow how that I koude pleyne
For Chauntėcleres drede and for his peyne.

   Certes, swich cry ne lamentaciòun
Was nevere of ladyes maad whan Yliòun   590
Was wonne, and Pirrus with his streitė swerd
Whan he hadde hent kyng Priam by the berd
And slayn hym (as seith us Eneydos),
As maden alle the hennes in the clos
Whan they had seyn of Chauntėcleer the sighte.   595
But sovėreynly dame Pertėlotė shrighte,
Ful louder than dide Hasdrubales wyf
Whan that hir housbonde haddė lost his lyf,
And that the Romayns haddė brend Cartáge—
She was so ful of torment and of rage   600
That wilfully into the fyr she sterte
And brende hirselven with a stedefast herte.

   O woful hennes, right so criden ye,
As, whan that Nero brendė the citée   (B 4560)
Of Romė, cryden senatòures wyves   605
For that hir husbondes losten alle hir lyves:
Withouten gilt this Nero hàth hem slayn.
Now wol I turnė to my tale agayn.

   This sely wydwe and eek hir doghtres two
Herden thise hennes crie and maken wo,   610
And out at dores stirten they anon,
And syen the fox toward the grovė gon,
And bar upon his bak the cok away,
And cryden, 'Out! harrow! and weylaway!

---

596 sovereynly] sodeynly *MS.*   605 senatours *MS.* ; the senatours
some MSS.   608 turne I wole *MS.*   609 This] The *some MSS.*

Ha! ha! the fox!' and after hym they ran,   615
And eek with staves many another man :
Ran Colle oure dogge, and Talbot. and Gerland,
And Malkyn, with a dystaf in hir hand ;
Ran cow and calf, and eek the verray hogges,
Sóre aferd for berkyng of the dogges   620
And shoutyng of the men and wommen eek,—
They ronné so hem thoughte hir herté breek ;
They yelleden as feendes doon in helle ;
The <u>dokes</u> cryden, as men wolde hem quelle ;   (B 4580)
The gees for feeré flowen over the trees ;   625
Out of the hyvé cam the swarm of bees,
So hydous was the noyse, a benedicitee !
Certes, he Jakké Straw and his meynée
Ne madé nevere shoutes half so shille
Whan that they wolden any Flemyng kille,   630
As thilké day was maad upon the fox.
Of bras they broghten bemes and of box,
Of horn, of boon, in whiche they blewe and powped,
And therwithal they skriked and they howped :
It semed as that hevene sholdé falle !   635
Now, goodé men, I prey yow, herkneth alle.

    Lo, how Fortúné turneth sodeynly
The hope and pryde eek of hir enemy !
This cok, that lay upon the foxes bak,
In al his drede unto the fox he spak   640
And seydé, 'Sire, if that I were as ye,
Yet sholde I seyn, as wys God helpé me !
"Turneth agayn, ye proudé cherles alle ;
A verray pestilence upon yow falle !   (B 4600)
Now I am come unto this wodes syde,   645
<u>Maugree</u> youre heed the cok shal heere abyde ;
I wol hym ete, in feith, and that anon." '

---

619 eek *om. MS.*   620 sore aferd] so fered *MS.* (*see note*).
622 They] The *MS.*   623 yolleden *MS.*   629 shille] shrille *some
MS.S.*   634 skriked] shriked *some MSS.*   638 eek *om. MS.*
642 sholde] wolde *MS.*   645 this] the *MS.*

The fox answérde, ' In feith, it shal be don.'—
And as he spak that word, al sodeynly
This cok brak from his mouth delyverly,   650
And heighe upon a tree he fleigh anon.
And whan the fox saugh that he was ygon,
    ' Allas! ' quod he, ' O Chauntécleer, allas!
I have to yow,' quod he, ' y-doon trespas,
In as muche as I maked yow aferd   655
Whan I yow hente and broght out of the yerd :
But, sire, I dide it in no wikke entente ;
Com doun, and I shal telle yow what I mente ;
I shal seye sooth to yow, God help me so ! '
    ' Nay, thanne,' quod he, ' I shrewe us bothe two, 660
And first I shrewe myself, bothe blood and bones,
If thou bigyle me any ofter than ones.
Thou shalt namoorè thurgh thy flaterye
Do me to synge and wynkè with myn eye ;   (B 4620)
For he that wynketh whan he sholdè see,   665
Al wilfully, God lat him nevere thee ! '
    ' Nay,' quod the fox, ' but God yeve hym meschaunce
That is so undiscreet of governaunce
That jangleth whan he sholdè holde his pees ! '
    Lo, swich it is for to be recchèlees   670
And necligent. and truste on flaterye !
    But ye that holden this tale a folýe
As of a fox, or of a cok and hen,
Táketh the moralité, goode men ;
For seint Poul seith that al that writen is   675
To oure doctríne it is y-write, ywis :
Táketh the fruyt and lat the chaf be stille.
Now goodè God, if that it be thy wille,
As seith my lord, so make us alle goode men,
And brynge us to his heighè blisse.   Amen.   680

Heere is ended the Nonnes Preestes tale.

652 ygon] gon *MSS. except Harl.* 7334.   656 out of the] into this
MS. and some others.   657 in] of *MS.*   662 any *om. some MSS.*
675 Poul] Paul *MS.*

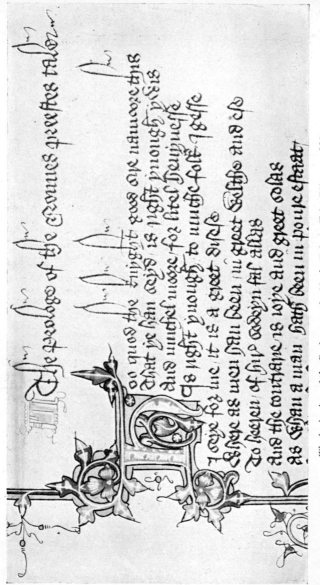

The beginning of the Prologue to the Nun's Priest's Tale, Ellesmere MS.

NOTES

The Monk's Tale

M. T. 737 *Cresus . . . Lyde*: Croesus, King of Lydia in Asia Minor, reputed to be the richest of men, was finally conquered by the Persians under Cyrus in 546 B.C. According to Herodotus, i. 87, he was saved by rain and spared by Cyrus. Chaucer's version comes from the *Roman de la Rose* (ed. Langlois, vol. iii, ll. 6489 ff.), but not from the part that Chaucer translated. The *Roman* in turn draws on the *Speculum Historiale* iii. 17, compiled by Vincent of Beauvais (d. 1264), or on the mythographical collections which are Vincent's source. Cp. Chaucer's translation of Boethius *de Consolatione Philosophiae* bk. ii, prose 2 :—Wystestow nat how Cresus, kyng of Lydyens, of whiche kyng Cirus was ful sore agast a lytil byforn,—that this rewliche Cresus was caught of Cirus and lad to the fyer to ben brend ; but that a rayn descendede down fro hevene that rescowyde hym.

M. T. 738 *hym dradde*: 'feared for himself'; 'dread' is commonly reflexive in early English.

M. T. 741 f *swich a revn . . . That*: modern English uses '*such . . . as*' or *such . . . that it*.

M. T. 743 'But still he had not the grace to be cautious', where *grace* = 'divine favour': it was not granted him to learn caution.

M. T. 745 f. *he kan nat stente For to begynne*: 'he cannot refrain from beginning'. Chaucer's choice between *for to* and *to* is usually governed by metrical convenience.

M. T. 750 *he mette*: 'he dreamed'; OE. *mǣtan* distinct from OE. *mētan* 'to meet'. *Mǣtan* is both personal, as here, and impersonal, as in *me mette* ll. 128, 132, &c. Cp. note to l. 12 below.

M. T. 753 *as that hym thoughte*: 'as it seemed to him'; see note to l. 12 below. Observe Chaucer's free use of compound connectives, which give ease and flow to his verse: *as that* = as ; *which that* 'who' 758, 768; *what that* 'what' 468 ; *wher(e) as* 'where' 6; 133; *ther as* 'where' 236; *whan that* 'when' 112, 122; *er that* 'before' 333 ; *syn that* 'since' 577; *though that* 'though' 207 ; *if that* 'if' 303; *how that* 'how' 237.

M. T. 753 ff. Herodotus iii. 124 says that the daughter of Poly-crates, another ruler famous for his prosperity, had such a dream before her father's murder (522 B.C.) (*Times Lit. Suppl.* 26 June 1924). The stories seem to have been fused in the Middle Ages.

M. T. 757–9 *to his doghter . . . he bad hire*: a broken construc-tion: *command*, which might have been used instead of *bad*, can be used with either construction.

M. T. 760 *bigan . . . expounde*: 'expounded'; cp. note to l. 307.

M. T. 761 *is to meene*: 'means'—the inflected infinitive, e. g. *is to mǣnanne*, has the same use in Old English.

M. T. 762 *Juppiter*: Jupiter as the god of rain and storm.

M. T. 764 *Tho been . . . for to seyn*: 'they express' or 'signify'; cp. note to l. 761.

M. T. 767 The metre is halting. If emendation is needed, the addition of *eek* 'also' after *and* does not harm a flat line.

M. T. 768 *Phanýe*: 'Phanie sa fille' in *Roman de la Rose*. I suspect that this unclassical name is due to misreading of a flourished *m* as *ph* in a MS.; cp. Vincent of Beauvais:—quod cum filiae suae *m*ane indicasset (*mane* 'at dawn' misread as *phane*, and interpreted as a proper name in apposition to *filiae*.)

M. T. 771 ff. 'Tragedy is nothing but this; nor can ⟨Tragedy⟩ lament and bewail in song (i. e. tragic verse) ⟨anything⟩ except ⟨this⟩: that Fortune &c.' Cp. Chaucer's *Boethius*, bk. ii, prose 2. 'What other thynge bywaylen the cryinges of tragedyes but oonly the dedes of Fortune, that *with unwar strook* overturneth the realmes of greet nobleye ?'; and the gloss thereon 'Tragedye is to seyn a dité of a prosperité for a tyme, that endeth in wrecchid-nesse'.

The Nun's Priest's Tale

1 ff. The Monk is a man of rank, and so it falls to the Knight, the chief of the company and the most courteous, to interrupt him. But there is some evidence that in the form of the Prologue without ll. 5–24 (see note to l. 16 ff.), the Host, not the Knight, was originally the interrupter.

1. Chaucer often repeats an expression that was common in the colloquial use of his time :—the Knight stops a quarrel between the Host and the Pardoner with ' Namore of this, for it is right ynough ' (C. 962) ; in the Knight's Tale Theseus twice parts Palamon and Arcite with ' Ho ! namore ' ; and Criseyde in *Troilus* iv, 1242 cries ' But ho ! for we han right ynough of this.'

2–5 'What you have said is quite enough indeed, and much more ⟨than enough⟩; for a little sadness is quite enough for many people, I am sure. For my part, I say it is very painful' &c.

12 *swich thyng*: so ll. 13, 45. This is the old construction; but *such a thing* appears early in Middle English; and *such things* has since taken its place in most uses.

it thynketh me: 'it seems to me'. The impersonal verb OE. *þyncan* 'to seem' became in many ME. forms indistinguishable from the personal verb, OE. *þencan* 'to think'. Chaucer still preserves several impersonal constructions which were lost in later English, e. g. *hym thoughte* 245, 248, 313; *hir neded* 68; *hem leste* 'it pleased them' (OE. *lystan*), *ne liste hym* 510; *hym deigned* 415 (here a French verb takes the construction); *it reweth me* 331 'I am sorry' (here *it* serves as a subject); cp. note to Monk's Tale 750 above. The loss of impersonal constructions is due to the dropping of inflexions in the noun. Thus in l. 346 Old English would have *Cēnhelm mǣtte* if the construction were personal, but *Cēnhelme* (dat.) *mǣtte* if it were impersonal. In Middle English the dative inflexion is lost except in pronouns; *Kenelm mette* may be either personal or impersonal; and as most verbs are personal, the small class of impersonals tends to disappear.

14 *Seintē Poules belle*: The ME. form *Poul(e)* is from Old French *Pol*; the modern *Paul* takes its spelling directly from Latin *Paulus*; cp. note to l. 675. While the city was still small (at this time its population was about 40,000), Old St. Paul's was a centre of civic life in a way that the modern cathedral cannot be. All the citizens would be within sound of its great bell, which was their common bell. So as early as the reign of Edward II they objected to the walling in of the eastern part of the churchyard, claiming it 'to be the place of assembly to their folkmotes, and that the great steeple there scituate was to that use, their common bell, which being there rung, al the inhabitants of the citie might heare and come together' (Stowe *Survey of London*, ed. Kingsford, i, p. 325). There is a certain appropriateness in the reference, for Chaucer himself, the Host, Pardoner, Manciple, Cook, and others, lived in or near the city.

16 ff. He refers to the last line of the Monk's Tale, and then to l. 771 ff. But this is begging a question :—

MSS. which end with Croesus have the tragedies in this order: Zenobia, *Peter of Spain, Peter of Cyprus, Bernabo Visconti, Ugolino of Pisa,* Nero, Holofernes, Antiochus, Alexander, Julius Caesar, Croesus. But the Ellesmere and other good MSS. have the four medieval stories (italicized) after Croesus. Defenders of the latter order explain, over-ingeniously, that the Host was drowsing (cp.

27

l. 31), and that his last recollections are of Croesus, some 100 lines before the Knight's interruption! Observe that all the references to Croesus are in ll. 5-24, which are not in MSS. like Corpus and Hengwrt. It has been argued (see Miss Hammond's *Bibliography*, pp. 241 ff.) that in its first state Chaucer's text did not contain these lines, and certainly there is nothing to account for their omission by accident. Perhaps the MSS. give confusedly two states of the text, both due to Chaucer: (i) Monk's Tale ending with Ugolino; Prologue without ll. 5-24; (ii) Monk's Tale ending with Croesus, and the much livelier Prologue containing the Host's jesting references, for which the moving tale of Ugolino gave no opportunity. It is hard now to judge the effect of the Prologue as if ll. 5-24 had never been written; but when they are absent l. 42 has more meaning, for the Host's ' rude speech and bold ' then appears for the first time. Chaucer may have felt that to stop the tale immediately after the story of Ugolino, which is a masterpiece, was inartistic; and that there was better ground for interruption if the Monk, after his modern examples which promised a speedy end to the series, wandered back to early Greek legend.

18 *no remédie*: Skeat took this as an echo of the Monk's opening lines:

> ' I wol biwaille in manere of Tragédie . . .
> And fillen so that ther nas no remédie.

But there *remédie* has quite a different sense. It is used in both places independently as a handy rime to *tragédie*.

23 *anoyeth*: ' wearies ' or ' is distasteful to '.

26 *daun Piers by youre name*: the circumlocution is not intended to be comic; cp. the Doctor's tale of Appius and Virginia (l. 213):

> ' Doghter ' quod he ' Virginia by thy name '.

Daun, Dan = ' sir ', Latin *dominus*; another form *Dom* is still used in addressing a monk. Chaucer also uses it as a respectful title for distinguished persons of antiquity, e. g. *daun Pharao* 367 ; and, playfully, *daun Russell* 568.

Piers is the French form of *Peter*, as in *Piers* Plowman and the modern surname *Pierce, Pearse*, &c. In the preamble to the Monk's Tale, the Host says he does not know the Monk's name:

> But by my trouthe I knowè nat youre name,—
> Wher shal I callè you my lord daun John,
> Or daun Thomas, or elles daun Albon ?

28 *nere clynkyng* &c.: ' were it not for the clinking ' &c. Cp. the description of the Monk in the Prologue:

> And whan he rood men myghte his brydel heere
> Gynglen in a whistlynge wynd als cleere
> And eek as loude as dooth the chapel belle, &c.

It has been noted (Introduction, § iv, end) that the frame of the Canterbury Tales is not very intimately connected with the stories; but the links are closely joined with the general Prologue, and probably most of the frame was written about the same time. See note to l. 37 ff.

32 Medieval roads were not good, and a rider in spring time had to pick his way through the mud-holes. There is another reference to the 'slough' in the preamble to the Manciple's Tale, when the drunken Cook falls off his horse.

34 *thise clerkes*: a common Middle English use of the demonstrative *this, these*, which does not imply that the 'clerkes' are particularized. We should say 'the learned'.

35 f. The Vulgate Bible has 'Ubi auditus non est non effundas sermonem' (Ecclus. xxxii. 6), which Chaucer translates in his tale of Melibeus: 'Ther as thou ne mayst have noon audience, enforce thee nat to speke' (B 2237); explaining: 'he that precheth to hem that listen nat heeren his wordes, his sermon hem anoieth'.

37 ff. 'And I know well that I have in me the stuff ⟨of a good listener⟩ if a thing is well told '. This leads up to the next line— if the Monk will tell some hunting story he will not find the Host unappreciative. The Monk's qualifications as a hunter are referred to in the Prologue, 178, 198 ff.

43 *the Nonnes Preest*: one of the three priests (Prol. 164) in attendance on the First Nun, i. e. the Prioress. Some prefer the form *Nonne Preest*, in which *Nonne* is the historical gen. sg. fem. < OE. *nunnan*; but by Chaucer's time the declension could follow the masculine nouns with a genitive in *-es*. There is no description of this Priest in the Prologue, but a few inferior MSS. contain an unfinished speech of the Host, which serves as Epilogue to the Nun's Priest's Tale and seems to be of Chaucer's own drafting. The following lines from it indicate that he was of the same brawny, florid, well-fed type as the Monk and the Friar; and give point to the Host's remarks about the wretched horse that had to carry him:

> Se whichė braunes hath this gentil Preest,
> So gret a nekke, and swich a largė breest!
> He loketh as a sperhauke with hise eyen!
> Him nedeth nat his colour for to dyghen
> With brasile ne with greyn of Portyngalė!
> Now, sire, fairė fallė yow for youre tale.

44 *neer*: 'nearer', still a true comparative of nigh.

sir John: an old nickname for a priest, who was properly addressed as *sir*. Here it appears to be a real name, cp. l. 54.

Note that few of the pilgrims are given surnames, which were a comparatively late development.   Harry Bailly the Host, and Chaucer himself are exceptions.

47. The reference to the Nun's Priest's scraggy horse may seem to be irrelevant; but it is introduced to make the picture sharp, and also implies that the Priest had to bear a good deal of chaff from his fellow-pilgrims because of his wretched mount.   Chaucer had an eye for horses : the Knight's were ' goode ' (Prol. 74), the Monk's ' in greet estaat (Prol. 203), the Clerk's nag was ' as leene as is a rake ' (287) ; the Shipman ' rood upon a rouncy, as he kouthe ' (390) ; the Wife of Bath ' upon an amblere ' (469) ; the Plowman ' upon a mere ' (541) ; the Reeve ' upon a ful good stot, That was al pomely grey, and hightè Scot ' (615) ; the Canon, who caught up the pilgrims at Boughton-under-Blee, had a horse of the same colour, sweating so ' that it wonder was to see ' ; and his Yeoman's horse was ' of foom al flekked as a pye ' (Canon Yeoman's Preamble).

50 *so moot I go !* : in early use *go* is frequently used in the narrow sense ' walk ' (see the juxtaposition to *ride* in the sixth verse quoted in the note to l. 113).   Hence ' so may I go ! ' = ' so may I enjoy the use of my legs ', and is exactly parallel to l. 534 (see note).

55 *somdeel stape in age* : somewhat advanced in age ', ' well on in years ' ; *stapen in age* occurs in Merchant's Tale, E 1514 ; and *stept in age* (*yeares*) is common in Elizabethan English.

57 *greve* : OE. has both *grǣf* > ME. *greve*, and *grāf* > ME. *grove*, l. 450.   Chaucer's rimes show *greve* only.   This is the wood of the *Roman de Renart* ; cp. ll. 570, 645 below.

59 *Syn thilkè day*, &c. : a mere formula for ' since her husband died ', with no implication that she had had more than one husband.

61 ' for her property and her revenues were small '.   In the Prologue 373 it is said of the burgesses : ' For catel hadde they ynogh and rente '.   *Catel* (modern *cattle*) and *chattel* are the Northern French and the Parisian French forms of the same word, Latin *capitale* ' principal ', ' property '.   In the sixteenth century *catel* was more and more restricted to live-stock, and from that time *chattel* came into use in the legal sense of movable possessions.

62 ' By careful management of such goods as God sent her she provided for (*foond*) herself, and her two daughters also.'

64 *and namo* : These empty phrases are very handy for rime-making.   Chaucer uses them less in the rimed couplet than in the more difficult stanza forms ; but he takes little pains to disguise

his tags. Many of the oaths and asseverations serve this purpose, e.g. *by that God above* 143, 151 ; *pardee* 162 ; *for Goddes owene love* 188 ; *for seinte charitee* 554 ; *so have I blis* 392 ; *so moot I thee* 210 (see note) ; *I wol nat lye* 179. Another kind is represented by *grete and lyte* 166. Some are adverbs : *for the nones* 567 ; *on a day* 347. Others are phrases like *quod he* 251, 277 ; *as ye may heere* 486 (cp. 497 f.) ; *I can sey you namoore* 203 ; *my tale is at an ende* 316. Notice also *Chauntecleer the faire* 453 ; *so free* 503. All are useful in spoken verse, which cannot be so concentrated as verse intended for a reader.

66 Her cottage was of two rooms—the *bower* or bedroom and the *hall* or living-room, this last not an elegant room, for Chantecler and his hens roosted there at night (l. 118). It was sooty from the open fire, which perhaps had a central hearth and no chimney.

70 *accordant to hir cote* : 'in keeping with her cottage'.

73 *hertes súffisàunce* : 'contentment'.

74 *The goute* &c.: 'gout did not stop her dancing at all (*nothyng*)'; i. e. she was not troubled by gouty feet.

76 *neither whit ne reed* : for the effects of these, see Pardoner's Tale, C. 562 ff. :—

> Now kepe yow fro the white and fro the rede,
> And namely fro the white wyn of Lepe
> That is to selle in Fysshstrete or in Chepe !
> This wyn of Spaigne crepeth subtilly
> In othere wynes growynge faste by,
> Of which ther ryseth swich fumositee
> That whan a man hath dronken draughtes thre,
> And weneth that he be at hoom in Chepe,
> He is in Spaigne right at the toune of Lepe !

79 f. 'broiled (*or* smoked ?) bacon and sometimes an egg or two, for she was, so to speak, a kind of dairy-keeper.'

80 *a maner deye* : a common construction, cp. Monk's Tale 771 above : *noon oother maner thyng*. Old English had a phrase with the genitive plural of *cynn* 'kin', e. g. *ealra cynna wildēor* 'wild beasts' *of all kinds*. With weakening of the inflexions in ME., this became *alle cynne bestes*, later *al kyn bestes*, and the true construction was no longer felt. When the French noun *maner(e)* was borrowed, it was properly construed with *of* : *al maner of bestes ; an manere of fishe* ; but it also took the construction of *kyn* : *al maner bestes ; a maner fish*. Ultimately *of* survived in both phrases : *all kinds of beasts ; what manner of man ?*

83 ff. There is a great deal of mock-heroics in this description, e. g. in l. 97, and it is worth comparing the descriptions in *Sir*

Thopas.   A late Middle English song runs (partly normalized) :—

I have a gentil cok
 Croweth me day ;
He doth me rysen erly
 My matynes for to say.

I have a gentil cok,
 Comen he is of gret ; [1]   [1] great stock.
His comb is of reed coral,
 His tayl is of jet.

I have a gentil cok,
 Comen he is of kynde ; [2]   [2] high lineage.
His comb is of reed coral,
 His tayl is of inde ; [3]   [3] dark blue.

His legges ben of asour [4]   [4] azure.
 So gentil and so smale ;
His spors arn of sylver whyt
 Into the wortewale ; [5]   [5] root.

His eyen arn of cristal
 Locken al in amber ;
And every nyght he percheth hym
 In myn ladyes chamber.
            (Brit. Mus. Sloane MS. 2593).

83 *heet Chauntecleer* : best taken as an ellipse of the relative (cp. the note to l. 133 f.), '⟨who⟩ was called Chantecler', where *heet* is the past tense of OE. *hātan*, used in the passive sense. The variant reading *highte* may either be construed in the same way (cp. *that hightē Malle* above) or as a past participle 'named'. For the complicated history of this verb, see N. E. D.

84 *of crowyng nas his peer* : 'there was not his equal in crowing'. Middle English often dispenses with the temporary subject 'there' or 'it' : e. g. *were gooaly* 'it would be good' 13 ; *nere clynkyng* 'were *it* not for the clinking' 28 ; *bifel*, 116, 235, 425, 'it happened' ; *happed so*, 221.

85 f. *orgón . . . gon* : the 3rd pl. *gon* (the 3rd sg. is *goth*) indicates that *orgon* is plural ; and Latin *organa* is a neuter plural because the instrument is made up of many pipes. But as there is no parallel in English for *orgon* plural, it is perhaps better to assume a careless construction here, influenced by the necessities of rime : 'pleasanter ⟨to hear⟩ than the sweet-toned organ,—⟨those⟩ that play in the church on feast-days '.

88 Note the scansion, *any‿abbey* (three syllables), which is not uncommon in Chaucer ; cp. note to l. 135.

89 ff. The equinoctial is the celestial equator, an imaginary circle through the heavens so drawn that the ecliptic (i. e. the circle representing the apparent annual course of the sun) cuts it at the equinoxes, 21 March and 23 September. Any point in the circumference of the equinoctial was supposed to be moving round it towards the west, completing the circle of 360° in 24 hours. Thus 15° of the equinoctial represents one hour. Now if we imagine a point in the equinoctial which ascends (i. e. rises above the horizon) at 6 a.m., then by 7 a.m. it will have travelled 15° along the equinoctial, and a second point in the equinoctial corresponding to 7 a.m. will be rising above the horizon. The Cock knew by nature the positions of each of these imaginary points, and so was able to crow every hour—according to sidereal time. But it was *local* sidereal time, depending on the longitude of the town in which the observer was ; so Chaucer has a purpose when he specifies *in thilke toun*. On the ability of cocks as astronomers Pliny in his *Natural History*, x. 21, says :—' Norunt sidera, et ternas distinguunt horas interdiu cantu ', &c.

90 Scan : *th'equynoxiàl* (five syllables). Skeat follows some MSS. in omitting *the*, but the invariable use of the article with *equinoxial* in Chaucer's *Astrolabe* seems decisive.

92 ' So that it could not be bettered ', ' perfectly '.

102 *as of colóurs* : ' in colour ' ; here ' as ' may be rendered ' in respect of ', but comparison with 227 *as for that nyght*, 319 *as for that day*, 234 *as in commúne* ' commonly ', shows that it has practically no meaning. Cp. note to l. 673.

103 *the faireste hewed on hir throte* : ' she who had the brightest feathers on her throat '. The mention of Pertelote's *throte* is suggested by the difficulty of finding rimes for her name. In the only other rime *throte* is used again (ll. 119 f.). We must picture her as an old-fashioned varicoloured barndoor-fowl, not one of the modern pure breeds.

104 *damoysele* : apparently disyllabic like modern *damsel*, and *fairè* takes the weak adjective inflexion, either because it is a quoted vocative (cp. 339), or because the weak adjective is preferred before proper names.

108 ff. ' She has in her keeping the heart of Chantecler ⟨whose⟩ every limb ⟨was⟩ bound fast ⟨by love⟩. He loved her so that his happiness was complete ' (lit. ' happiness came (was) to him with it '). But this paraphrase of the first sentence is more logical than the original. See note to l. 113.

111 *swich a joye was it* : this is a natural enough form of

exclamation in modern English, but where there is no correlative clause, Middle English uses *which a joy*! The earliest examples of *such* in this sense in N. E. D. are from the sixteenth century, so perhaps the construction is broken here.

hem : the Cock is ordinarily the songster ; but Pertelote and Chantecler are no mere Cock and Hen—they are a lady and her knight. Hence they sing an old English song ' in sweete accord '. Elsewhere Chantecler has a shirt (l. 354) and a beard (l. 154) ; and Pertelote's ideal husband is the same as any other woman's (l. 146 ff.). This trick of giving the animals human attributes is carried to great lengths in the later Reynard stories, where they ride horses, fight in armour, &c. Chaucer uses it more delicately to extract the maximum of fun from the story.

113 *My lief is faren in londe* : ' My love has gone away '. Skeat (*Athenæum*, 24 Oct. 1896, p. 566) found a verse of this song in Trinity College, Cambridge MS. R. 3. 19, and it must have been running in Chaucer's head when he wrote ll. 108–9 :—

> My lefe ys faren in lond ;
> Allas ! why ys she so ?
> And I am so sore bound [1]   [1] ? *read* in bonde.
> I may nat com her to.
> *She hath my hert in hold*
> Wherever she ryde or go,
> With trew love a thousandfold.

121 *as man that* : ' like one who ' ; cp. 512, 557. Here *man* is used as an indefinite pronoun, like OE. *man* ' one ', but it is not a continuation of that use.

125 *Ye been a verray slepere* : ' A fine sleeper you are ! '

127 f. ' I pray you don't be offended. I dreamt I was in such trouble just now that ', &c.

128 *By God!* Like French *mon Dieu*, German *mein Gott*. Such oaths and asseverations were common form in Chaucer's time, despite the efforts of preachers (cp. Pardoner's Tale C. 629 ff.), and their frequency weakened their force. They were swept out of literary use by the Puritan reform. Cp. note to l. 64.

130 *recche aright* : ' interpret favourably ', in the sense ' give a fortunate issue to '.

133 f. ' Where I saw a beast ⟨that⟩ was like a dog, and that would have seized me and killed me '. In early English the relative is often not expressed, but relation is indicated by juxtaposing the principal and relative clauses ; so l. 409 ' He hadde founde *a corn lay* in the yerd ' = ' that lay '. Cp. note to l. 83.

135 *han* : I retain the reading of the more careful MSS. against

wolde han of the independent Corpus group of MSS.; but the choice is difficult. If *han* is original, *wolde* may be miscopied from the line above. If *wolde han* is original, *wolde* may have been discarded by some early corrector as unnecessary to the sense and the metre. Yet Chaucer would probably scan *body and* as two syllables, not three. Cp. *body is* (two syllables) 253; *many a* (two syllables) 209, &c.; and note to l. 88.

139 *his snowté smal*: 'his muzzle slim'. Cp. l. 542 n.

140 *his look*: it is hard to decide whether this means 'the expression of his eyes', or the whole appearance of the beast— 'the look of him'.

142 *hertélees*: 'coward', cp. l. 145.

144 *myn . . . my*: note that *myn* is used before a vowel or initial *h*; *my* before a consonant.

148 ff. So Hercules told Hypsipyle that Jason was 'wyse, hardy, secree and ryche' and excelling in 'fredome', *Leg. Good Women* 1528 ff.; and the merchant's wife in the Shipman's Tale B. 1363 ff. says all women require husbands to be 'Hardy and wise, and riche, and therto free'. *Avauntours* 'boasters', with reference to those who brag of their success in love; cp. *Troilus* ii. 724 ff.

151 f. *By that God above! . . . love*: note the repetition of l. 143 and the rime. To introduce *above* was almost the only way of riming *love*, for *dove* still had a long vowel in Chaucer's day, and though *shove* as a past participle would rime, its meaning lessened its usefulness.

156 *vanitee*: in its etymological sense 'emptiness'.

157 ff. On *compleccioun*, *humour*, *repleccioun* (which can also mean 'over-eating' as in l. 71) see note to l. 160 ff. *Fume* is noxious vapours, supposed to arise from the stomach and trouble the brain.

160 ff. Pertelote's diagnosis is minutely adapted to the symptoms. Diseases were supposed to arise from the excess (*repleccioun*) of one or more of the four 'humours' or bodily moistures: *cholera* or yellow-red bile in choleric persons, *melancholia* or black bile in the melancholic, *blood* in the sanguine, *phlegm* in the phlegmatic; and the particular blending of these humours in any one person determined his 'temperament' or 'complexion'—both meaning properly 'blending'. Further, the excess of a humour produced dreams in which the corresponding colour occurred—the choleric dreamt of fiery red things (163 ff.); the melancholic of black things (167 ff.); Chantecler has dreamt of a beast *betwixe yelow and reed* with black markings. It follows that he is suffering from excess of yellow-red and black bile, and that the treatment is physic to purge him of *colere and maléncolýe* (l. 180).

161 *comth of the grete* : the Ellesmere MS. has the uncontracted *cometh*, which often disturbs the rhythm in MSS. of Chaucer (e. g. in Pardoner's Tale C. 656 ; *Parlement of Fowles*, ll. 23, 25) ; and also the unmetrical and ungrammatical *the greet*, where the weak adjectival form *grete* must be restored. Such a line shows that even the best MSS. cannot be relied on to reproduce the details of Chaucer's own manuscript. They were copied in the fifteenth century, when the grammatical forms on which his metre depends had to some extent broken down.

163 f. *dreden . . . of* : the construction might seem to favour the variant reading *dremen* for *dreden* ; but in Middle English *dreden* can take *of* governing the thing dreaded ; cp. M.T. 738 above.

164–6 'Fire with red flames' and 'red beasts' are obvious dreams arising from the fiery 'cholera'. *Conteks*, 'quarrels', are scenes of violence, for Contek is personified 'with blody knyf and sharpe manace' (Knight's Tale A. 2003). The commonest dogs (*whelpes*) may have been of the yellowish-red kind, but more likely a dogfight troubled the sleeper. It is not easy to see the appropriateness of *arrows*, unless fiery arrows are meant.

169 *beres* should be two syllables, so that the variant reading in the footnote is smoother.

170 Either (i) the relative is omitted : or else black devils ⟨who⟩ try to seize them' (cp. l. 165 and note to l. 133 f.) ; or (ii) the construction is broken = ' or else ⟨they dream that⟩ black devils', &c.

172 *werken . . ful wo* : the phrase occurs elsewhere, e. g. *Havelok* 2453 (cp. ibid. 611). *Wo* is properly a noun, and is construed with a dative, e. g. *him was wo*. When the dative was a noun without inflexion, (*John was wo*), *John* was understood as the subject, and *wo* as an adjective 'woeful', with which the intensive adverb *ful* could be used—*John was ful wo*. In *werken ful wo*, it seems that *ful* has become attached to the noun *wo*, because it was often used with *wo* adj. Translate 'cause much distress'.

174 f. *Catoun* : Dionysius Cato, to whom the *Disticha Catonis*, a fourth-century collection of moral sayings in Latin verse, are attributed. It was in regular use as a school-book up to the seventeenth century, and was prescribed in the statutes of many old grammar schools. The saying referred to is in Book ii, distich 32 :

> *Somnia ne cures*, nam mens humana quod optat
> Dum vigilat sperat, per sompnum cernit idipsum.

ne do no fors of dremes 'attach no importance to dreams' translates the italicized words. There is an Old English and several Middle English versions of the Distichs. See Wells, *Manual*, pp. 378, 822.

177 *as taak*: 'take'. This form of the imperative with *as* (sometimes *so*) is very common in Chaucer, but has yet to be recorded outside his works. It is a polite form in which *as*, *so* make the command less abrupt, and seems to be modelled on the subjunctive 'as (so) help me God', &c.

182 *Though in this toun is noon apothecarie*: a precise detail, but the rimes to some extent steer the sense. So *tarie*: *apothecarie* rime in the Pardoner's Tale, C. 851 f.

183 *techen*: 'direct'.

186 'Which have naturally (*by kynde*) from their special virtue (*propretee*) ⟨the power⟩ to purge you, upwards and downwards (*bynethe and eek above*)'.

189 *coleryk of complecciõun*: the description of the Cock, with his coral-red comb and feathers of burnished gold, is sufficient warrant for this; see note to l. 160 ff. *Complexion* now has the narrow sense 'colour & texture of the skin of the face', the face being regarded as the index of the 'complexion' or blending of humours in the body.

190 f. *Waré*, &c.: 'Beware lest the sun, as his altitude increases (during summer), should find you full of hot humours'. The humours were classified as hot and cold, dry and moist. Choler was hot and dry, Blood was hot and moist.

193 *fevere terciàne*: a fever increasing in violence every other day, as distinct from a *quotidian*, in which the crises came every day, and a *quartan* in which it came every third day. On the old way of reckoning what we should call every *second* day was called every *third* (*tertianus*).

197–9 After the worms taken as a digestive (i. e. a medicine to promote digestion of food, here chosen with an eye to the habits of birds), the following herbs were used as laxatives:—

lawriol: the spurge laurel (*Daphne laureola*). *A Boke of the Properties of Herbes* (1550) says: 'it wyll make a man laxatyve and it is good to purge a man of flewme and of the coler.'

centáure: the lesser centaury (*Erythraea centaurium*) used to purge choler and phlegm.

fumetère: 'fumitory' (*Fumaria officinalis*). Another purge for melancholy: 'it openeth the lyver and it clereth a man's blode.'

ellébor: there are two kinds, the black (*Helleborus niger*) 'called blacke . . . because it purgeth the coleryke blacke humours' according to *The Great Herball of Treviris* (1526); and the white (*Veratrum album*) which was particularly used against phlegm and 'purgeth upward by vomyte' *ibid*.

katapucè: According to the authority just quoted 'it is the frute or sede of a tree that is called catapucia, and whan catapucia

is founde in receptes, it is meant the fruyte and not the herbe . . .
It hath vertu to purge the flewmes principally, and secondly the
melancholyke & coleryke humours. It hath might to *purge above*
because it causeth wind that restrayneth the humoures upwarde.'

gaitrys beryis: apparently berries of the buckthorn (*Rhamnus
catharticus*), a strong purgative, formerly considered effective
against choler. In modern dialects *gaiter berries* or *gattridge
berries* are usually the berries of Dogwood (*Cornus sanguinea*), but
its berries have no medicinal use, and are very like those of buckthorn. Neither kind can be gathered in May.

198 *that groweth there*: a forced rime, but *there* can be referred
back to *in oure yeerd* in l. 185.

200 *herbe-yve*: perhaps the buck's horn, *coronopus*, OFr. *herbe
yve*. Oddly enough, though the rhythm shows that *yve* is a mono-
syllable, the commentators have taken it as a kind of *ivy*, OE. *īfig*,
which must be two syllables, and have been hard put to it to explain the medical use of ivy. Buck's horn has the medicinal properties of the plantains, which were given to cure jaundice and
tertian fevers.

in oure yeerd ther mery is: another of Chaucer's forced rimes.
He is often driven to this device of riming the plural ending with
the verb *is* (cp. 155 f., 469 f.) ; and *beryis* is a troublesome word,
for which rimes were almost impossible to find ; *ther* = 'where' :
translate ' in that pleasant spot in our yard ', or possibly ' in our
pleasant yard '.

201 Note the scansion :

'Pékke͜hem ùp | ríght as | they grówe, | and éte | hem ýn '.

202 *for youre fader kyn* : ' for the sake of your father's stock ' ;
where *fader* is a correct old form of the genitive sg. Often a mere
tag ; but Chantecler was proud of his race, and the Fox played on
the same string (529 ff.).

210 *so moot I thee!* : 'so may I prosper !' OE. *þēon* 'to thrive';
cp. 666 and note to l. 50.

213 ff. On the significance of dreams, see *Hous of Fame* (at the
beginning), *Roman de la Rose* (the beginning), and *Troilus* v. 358 ff.
Curiosity about their interpretation gave rise to an important branch
of popular literature—the ' dream-books ', of which the medieval
examples trace back to Byzantine Greek sources. There are texts
in Anglo-Saxon and in Middle English ; but beyond the general
statement that to dream of being attacked by a beast, or indeed to
dream of any quadruped, meant trouble, they do not help much.

217 ' The actual result (*preevè*) shows it, in practice ' ; if *preevè*
means ' test of experience ', the general sense is the same.

218 *oon of the gretteste auctour* : so the best MSS. In Middle
English there is a fairly common construction 'one the greatest
(man)' like Latin *unus maximus*. In late Middle English 'one *of*
the greatest (men)', i. e. 'one *from among* the greatest', tends to
replace it. Here we seem to have a transitional stage, with *of* from
the new construction and the singular *auctour* from the old.
Cp. Melibeus (B. 2868) 'ye knowen wel that *oon of the gretteste* and
moost sovereyn *thyng* that is in this world'. The author referred
to is either Cicero, who in *De Divinatione* i, c. 27, tells both stories
in reverse order, or Valerius Maximus who has the second story at
i, c. 8 (3) and the first at i, c. 8 (10) of his *Facta et Dicta Memora-
bilia*. Valerius borrows from Cicero, and it is hard to say which
author Chaucer's free versions derive from, for where he seems
nearer to Valerius, the chances of coincidence in variation from
Cicero are great. Here are the two versions :—

<table>
<tr><td>Cicero i. 27.</td><td>Valerius Maximus i. c. 8 (3).</td></tr>
<tr><td>

(i) Unum de Simonide : qui
cum ignotum quendam pro-
iectum mortuum vidisset
eumque humauisset, haberet-
que in animo nauem con-
scendere, moneri visus est ne
id faceret ab eo quem sepul-
tura adfecerat ; si nauigauis-
set, eum naufragio esse peri-
turum ; itaque Simonidem
rediisse, periisse ceteros qui
tum nauigauissent.
</td><td>

(i) Longe indulgentius dii in
poeta Simonide cuius salutarem
inter quietem admonitionem con-
silii firmitate roborarunt. Is enim
cum ad litus nauem appulisset in-
humatumque corpus iacens sepul-
turae mandasset, admonitus ab eo
ne proximo die nauigaret, in terra
remansit. Qui inde soluerant,
fluctibus et procellis in conspectu
eius obruti sunt ; ipse laetatus est
quod vitam suam somnio quam naui
credere maluisset. Memor autem
beneficii elegantissimo carmine ae-
ternitati consecrauit, melius illi et
diuturnius in animis hominum se-
pulcrum constituens quam in de-
sertis et ignotis harenis struxerat.
</td></tr>
<tr><td></td><td style="text-align:center">ibid., c. 8 (10).</td></tr>
<tr><td>

(ii) Alterum ita traditum,
clarum admodum somnium :
cum duo quidam Arcades
familiares iter una facerent
et Megaram venissent, alte-
rum ad coponem deuertisse,
ad hospitem alterum ; qui ut
cenati quiescerent concubia
nocte visum esse in somnis
ei qui erat in hospitio, illum
alterum orare ut subueniret,
quod sibi a copone interitus
</td><td>

(ii) Proximum somnium etsi paulo
est longius, propter nimiam tamen
euidentiam ne omittatur impetrat.
Duo familiares Arcades iter una
facientes Megaram uenerunt,
quorum alter se ad hospitem con-
tulit, alter in tabernam meritoriam
deuertit. Is qui in hospitio erat
</td></tr>
</table>

pararetur : eum primo per-
territum somnio surrexisse,
dein cum se conlegisset idque
visum pro nihilo habendum
esse duxisset, recubuisse ;
tum ei dormienti eundem
illum visum esse rogare ut,
quoniam sibi viuo non sub-
uenisset, mortem suam ne
inultam esse pateretur : se
interfectum in plaustrum a
copone esse coniectum et su-
pra stercus iniectum; petere
ut mane ad portam adesset,
priusquam plaustrum ex op-
pido exiret. Hoc vero eum
somnio commotum mane bu-
bulco praesto ad portam
fuisse, quaesisse ex eo quid
esset in plaustro : illum per-
territum fugisse, mortuum
erutum esse, coponem re pate-
facta poenas dedisse.

vidit in somniis comitem suum
orantem ut sibi coponis insidiis
circumuento subueniret : posse enim
celeri eius adcursu se imminenti
periculo subtrahi. Quo visu exci-
tatus prosiluit tabernamque, in qua
is deuersabatur, petere conatus est.
Pestifero deinde fato eius humanis-
simum propositum tamquam super-
uacuum damnauit et lectum ac
somnum repetit. Tunc idem ei
saucius oblatus obsecrauit ut,
quoniam vitae suae auxilium ferre
neglexisset, neci saltem ultionem
non negaret : corpus enim suum a
copone trucidatum tum maxime
plaustro ferri ad portam stercore
coopertum. Tam constantibus fami-
liaris precibus compulsus protinus
ad portam cucurrit et plaustrum,
quod in quiete demonstratum erat,
conprehendit coponemque ad capitale supplicium perduxit.

Probably Chaucer had the stories neither from Cicero nor Valerius,
but from some medieval collection in which the classical source was
quoted. Miss Petersen *On the Sources*, &c. has suggested use of
Libri Sapientiae, by Robert Holkot (d. 1349) which contains both
stories (they are not connected) with a reference to Valerius, as
well as a good deal of matter on dreams, &c. that has close parallels
in Chaucer. But the range of material in the Middle Ages was
narrow, the topic was popular, and the chance of coincidence great.
It is possible, but not likely, that Chaucer drew upon Holkot.

219-34 All this is expanded to suit medieval conditions from the
simple statement in Cicero and Valerius that two men on their way
to Megara spent the night, one with a friend, the other at an inn.

221-3 'a town where so many people were gathered, and ⟨which⟩
was so short of accommodation that ', &c.

231 *fer in a yeerd* : 'far down a yard '; the point is that he was
far away from the house and the street, and therefore far from help.

250 *morwe-tyde* : 'morning ', cp. 464, 488. That *tomorwe* 315
is 'to-morrow *morning* ', not simply 'to-morrow ' in the modern
sense, appears from l. 309.

251 *the westgate* : the medieval town was regularly walled against
enemies, and the gates were often called after the quarter in which

Notes

they were placed. So the writer of the *Ayenbyte* is called Dan Michel of *Northgate*; and *Eastgate, Westgate, Southgate* are still common personal names.

254 *do thilke carte arresten*: 'cause (somebody) to arrest it', 'have it stopped'—a regular ME. use of *do*+infinitive.

258 *truste*: for the imperative plural Chaucer uses indifferently the normal form in *-eth*, e. g. *herkneth* 636, *turneth* 643; or a shorter form in *-e*, as here. A good example of the alternatives is Clerk's Tale, ll. 7–20.

260 *in*: 'inn'.

263 *answérede*: MS. *answerde*, but it is better not to assume that *e* before *hym* is syllabic. Cp. the quotation in the note to l. 673 ff., where the MS. again has *answerde*; and note to l. 318 f.

266 *gan fallen in suspecioun*: 'became suspicious'; cp. l. 307 n. Note the variant reading.

270 *as it were*: oddly used, perhaps to indicate the ostensible purpose, the real purpose being to hide the body. But the suspicious construction, and the occurrence of *wente* in so many good MSS. (see footnote), cannot be neglected: the reading

A dóng-|carte wénte | as it wére | to dóng | è lónd

is possibly right.

273 *with an hardy herte*: = *boldely*, 254.

276 *gapyng upright*: 'face upwards (*upright*) with mouth open' i. e. with the jaw dropped in death. Note the scansion

And ín | this cárte | héere he lith | gápyng | upríght |

as if to suggest hurried and excited speech.

280 *What sholde I . . . ?*: 'Why should I . . . ?'

284 ff. Opposite these lines the Ellesmere MS. has *Auctor*, indicating that they are to be read as a comment by Chaucer.

286 *Mordre wol out*: an instance of the ellipse of a verb of motion after *will*, which was still common in Shakespeare's time, e. g. 'I will myself into the pulpit first', *Julius Caesar*, III. i. 236. The proverb occurs again in the Prioress's Tale B. 1766.

287 *abhomynable*: the spelling with *h* is due to a false etymology, *ab homine*, as if 'alien to man's nature'. The true derivation is Latin *ab-ōminari*, 'to turn away from as of ill-omen'.

291 *this my conclusioùn*: common in Middle English for the fuller expression *this is*; so *Parlement of Fowles* 620, *this my conclusion*. The copyists sometimes inserted *is* where the rhythm shows that it should be omitted, e. g. Franklin's Tale F. 889

As kepe | my lord! | this *is* my | conclu|sioùn;

Clerk's Tale 56

> But this | *is* his ta|lè which | that ye | may heere.

293 f. *pyned . . . engýned*: 'tortured . . . racked'—methods of securing a confession which were long considered a necessary part of judicial procedure.

297 *to drede*: 'to be dreaded', the Old English gerundial infinitive *to drǣdanne*. Chaucer uses *for to drede* in the same sense when it is metrically convenient, e. g. l. 343. Cp. note to Monk's Tale 745 f.

299 *right in the nextè chapitre after this*: in Cicero Chaucer's second story precedes the first ; in Valerius Maximus it is several sections earlier (cp. note to l. 218). Either Chaucer is writing from memory, or he took the stories from some intermediary in which they were rearranged. Holkot has them in the same order as Chaucer, but they are not close together.

301 *Two men that*: Chaucer gets lost in the succession of subordinate clauses beginning with *that*, and there is no formal predicate to *two men*.

307 *gan chaunge and blew*: 'changed and blew'—a good example of *gan* + infinitive used to express the simple preterite ; cp. ll. 112, 237, 266, 408, 516. *Bigan* is sometimes used in the same way with no inchoative sense, e. g. Monk's Tale 760. It is often difficult to decide whether the best rendering is the preterite, e. g. ll. 120, 262, 273, 321.

309 *casten hem* : 'made up their minds', 'resolved'—an earlier example of this reflexive use of *cast* than those in N.E.D.

310 (*herkneth*) : the verse is complete without this word : but such extra-metrical asides are too common in Middle English to be rejected off-hand : cp. *Sir Orfeo* 419

> ' O lord,' (he seyd), ' ʒif it thi wille were '.

There is an instance in Chaucer's *Legend of Good Women* 1338

> (And seyde) 'O swetè cloth, while Juppiter hit leste ',

which Skeat emends by omitting *swetè*, and the Globe edition by altering *Juppiter* to *Jove*. The licence belongs to the tradition of spoken verse, where the minstrel could by his tone distinguish the intrusive words from the verse proper.

311 f. *that oon . . . hym mette*: *mette* 'dreamt' is either personal or impersonal (note to Monk's Tale 750 above), and here it seems to be both. Probably this is a loose construction ; but *that oon . . . hym* may be taken together as a dative equivalent.

312 *agayn the day*: 'just before dawn'. Dreams after midnight were regarded as more significant than dreams early in the night. Cp. ll. 116, 235.

42

318 f. *preyede* . . . *preyede* : MS. *preyde* . . . *preyde*, and the editors make up the metre by assuming that the final *-e* of *preyde* is syllabic, though it should normally be elided before *hym* as in Man of Law's Tale 1084

> She preyd|e‿hym eek | he wold|ē by | no weye,

or B. 1718   This preyd|e‿he hym | to cón|strue and | declare.

But the same form *preyde* disturbs the normal scansion over and over again, e. g. Miller's Tale A. 3838

> And that | he prey|de hem | for god|des love ;

E. 680   Save this | she prey|de hym | that if | he mighte ;

D. 959   He prey|de hire | that to | no cre|atùre ;

C. 853   And prey|de hym | that he | hym wold|ē selle ;

E. 1631   And prey|de hem | to la|boure in | this nede ;

F. 311   And prey|de hym | to tell|e‿his go|vernaunce.

In D. 895   So long|ē prey|den | the King | of grace,
it is impossible to get round the difficulty by assuming syllabic *-e* in hiatus, so the editors read *preyēden*, and this is the solution of all such passages. Chaucer used two forms, *preyēde* and *preyde*, but the scribes have usually altered *preyede* to *preyde*, spoiling the metre ; cp. note to l. 263. This choice of forms was one of the great advantages of Middle English for easy narrative : Chaucer can use *slawe* 248 or *slayn* 256 as past participles of *slee(n)*, *toos* 565 or *toon* 96 as plurals of *too*, as it suits his rime ; ' *ther as* he lay ' 236 or ' *ther* I lye 239 ; *for to drede* 343 or *to drede* 297 n. ; the pp. *writen* 675 or *y-write* 676 ; the infinitive in *-en* (*gronen in* 120) or in *-e* (*grone in* 124), according as it suits his rhythm.

320 *that lay by his beddes syde* : i. e. they shared a room ; but Chaucer says so because it is convenient to repeat the rime of 313 f.

321 *scorned him ful faste* : ' poured scorn upon him '.

323 ' that I will delay doing my business '.   This verb *let* < OE. *lettan* is distinct from *let* ' allow, &c.' < OE. *lǣtan*.   Its intransitive sense seems to arise from a reflexive use, ' hinder myself '.

326. *alday* : ' every day ', ' always ', ' constantly '.   *Owls* were birds of ill-omen, but *apes* are probably mentioned for no better reason than the favourite rime with *japes*.

328 *of thyng that nevere was, ne shal* : supply ' be ' ; the ellipse is common after *shal*, e. g. Knight's Tale A. 1359 f.

> So muchē sorwe hadde nevere creatùre
> That is or *shal*.

Thing can be used in Middle English in an indefinite sense either with or without the indefinite article.   In modern English we must say ' a thing ' or ' things '.

331 *and have good day*: 'so farewell'—a form of leave-taking.

335 *casuelly*: 'by some mischance'.

338 *tyde*: 'time', not 'tide' here.

344 ff. King Cēnwulf (*Kenulphus*) of Mercia (*Mercenrike*) died in the year 819. He is said to have been succeeded by his son Kenelm (OE. Cēnhelm), then only seven years old (cp. l. 351), who was murdered in Clent forest at the instigation of his sister Cwenthryth. Nothing is heard of St. Kenelm in documents earlier than the late tenth century, when his cult seems to have become active. His vision of a beautiful tree, which he climbed, only to find it cut away beneath him by his attendants, is not reported in the earlier authorities (such as Florence of Worcester, d. 1118), and is no doubt an invention, like the story of the psalter, long preserved at Winchcomb, which bore the marks where the eyes of his wicked sister Cwenthryth fell out as she read Psalm 108 to curse his funeral ; or the story of the dove that flew to Rome and laid on the altar a slip of parchment with the words

> On Clent Cubach Kenelme, kinges bern,
> Lith under thorn, hevede bireved.

The legend may be read in the South English Legendary (Early English Text Soc.), p. 345 ff.

345 *the noble kyng*, &c.; in apposition to *Kenulphus*, not to *Kenelm*.

350 f. *to kepe hym weel For traisoun* : 'to guard himself well *against* treason'—a fairly common ME. use of *for*.

352 *litel talē hath he toold of*: 'he attached little importance to '.

354 *I haddē levere than my sherte* : cp. note to l. 111. In Old English the expression was *mē is lēofre* 'it is dearer to me'; but in ME. a new form arises : *I hadde levere* ' I would hold it dearer ' ; and later the phrase *I hadde rather* was modelled upon it.

355 *legende*: in its strict sense, Latin *legenda* 'thing(s) to be read ', modern 'lesson' in church. On a saint's day, his story, (or extracts from it) was read as part of the church service.

357 *Macrobeus, that writ the Avisioun*, etc. : Cicero's *Somnium Scipionis* (or Vision of Scipio Africanus Minor, d. B.C. 128), part of the sixth book of his *de Republica*, is known by the quotations embedded in the commentary of Macrobius Theodosius (*circa* 400 A.D.). Scipio relates a vision in which his grandfather, Scipio Africanus Major, appeared to him and, leading him to the Milky Way, showed him that he would conquer Carthage. Macrobius begins the commentary with a classification of dreams and their degrees of significance, and it was this, with the philosophic and astronomical explanations, that attracted medieval readers. It had

some influence in making the dream a favourite setting for medieval works, e. g. Dante's *Divina Commedia*, the *Roman de la Rose*; and in English *Pearl*, the *Vision of Piers Plowman*; Chaucer's *Dethe of Blaunche*, *Parlement of Fowles*, *Hous of Fame*.   In each of the three last poems Macrobius is referred to, and in *Parlement of Fowles* 29 ff., where Scipio is Chaucer's guide, there is a fairly full account of the *Somnium Scipionis*.   Another very important passage for comparison is the beginning of the *Roman de la Rose* (translated by Chaucer), which probably suggested the reference.

358. *In Affrike*: Scipio was on a visit to the African prince Massinissa when he saw the vision : cp. *Parlement of Fowles* 36 f.

> First telleth it, whan Scipioun was come
> In Affrik, how he mettè Massynisse . . .

362 *of Daniel* : 'concerning Daniel ', like Latin *de*.   See Daniel i. 17 and the following chapters.

364 *Joseph* : See Genesis xl, xli.

365 *Wher* : a short form of *whether*, cp. l. 369. It may introduce either an indirect or a direct question, and in the latter case it cannot be translated by *whether*.   In l. 369 the question is perhaps direct : ' did *they* feel no consequences of dreams ? '

370 *seken actes* : ' search the histories '—Latin *acta* 'things done'.

372 *Lo Cresus* : Observe how *lo* is used as an equivalent of *looke*, though they are of different origin : OE. *lā* 'lo!'; OE. *lōca* (imperative of *lōcian*) 'look'.   The reference to Croesus, without any mention of the Monk's Tale, is an indication that the Nun's Priest's Tale was not originally written to follow the Monk's Tale in a larger work.   See Introd. § iv, end, and note to Monk's Tale 737.

375 *Andromacha* : This dream is not in Homer.   The medieval Troy story is a romance derived from the spurious Latin histories of Dares the Phrygian (fourth century A.D.) and Dictys of Crete. Life was infused into their narrative by Benoît de St. More in his French *Roman de Troie* (about 1184); and in 1287 Guido de Columnis abridged Benoît's poem to make the Latin prose *Historia Troiana*, from which derive the Middle English alliterative *Destruction of Troy*, Lydgate's *Troy Book* and the Laud *Troy Book*.   The most famous story of the Troy cycle, Troilus and Cressida, came to Chaucer from Guido through Boccaccio.   The dream of Andromache is in Dares c. xxiv ; in Guido bk. xxi ; in the alliterative *Destruction of Troy* ll. 8425 ff., &c.

376 *sholdé lese* : 'was destined to lose '.

384 *I may nat dwelle* : Chantecler must not neglect his duty of crowing at daybreak.   See note to 546 f.

389 *venymes* : it is hard to decide between the plural noun and the adjective *venymus* which is found in some MSS.

45

395 *so scarlet-reed aboute youre eyen* : Pertelote, as the ideal hen, was no doubt a great layer (cp. Pinte's reputation Introd. § ii), and the pinkish skin on a hen's head goes bright scarlet when she is laying.

397 *Al so siker as* In principio : 'as true as the gospel'. *In principio* (*erat Verbum*), 'In the beginning (was the Word)', is the opening of the Gospel of St. John, and the short name for its first fourteen verses, which were the most popular gospel-excerpt of the later Middle Ages, and were supposed to have extraordinary powers. The Friars, quick to catch the taste of the people, recited them from house to house (see Prologue 254—So plesaunt was his *In principio*). Hence Chantecler refers to them as gospel-truth *par excellence*, and declares that the following sentence is as true.

398 *Mulier est hominis confusio*: i. e. 'Woman is man's confusion'. A favourite form of medieval literature was the series of questions and answers, some instructive and some in the nature of riddles. Such are the dialogues of Solomon and Marcolf; Solomon and Saturn (in Anglo-Saxon) ; the Emperor Hadrian and Ritheus ; Hadrian and Epictetus, &c. This particular answer is found in the dialogue attributed to Hadrian and the philosopher Secundus, which is reported by Vincent of Beauvais (see note to Monk's Tale 737 above) in his *Speculum Historiale* x. 70–1 ; and it is often found separate (see *Modern Language Notes* xxxv, p. 479 ff.):— Hadrian asks: 'Quid est mulier ?' and Secundus answers : 'Hominis confusio, insaturabilis bestia, continua sollicitudo, indesinens pugna, viri continentis naufragium, humanum mancipium'. Chantecler quotes the first description, and takes advantage of Pertelote's lack of Latin to give it an opposite meaning. The Bible (Ecclus. xxv, xxvi) gives the model for the balancing of woman's qualities.

406 *fly* : 'flew' past tense; the forms *fleigh* (573, 651), *fley*, *fly* are all possible in the fourteenth century, representing one development of the OE. pa. t. sg. *flēah* ; another development from the same form is *flaugh* 465; and the plural *flowen* 625 takes its vowel from the pa. t. pl. OE. *flugon*.

410 *real* and *roial* (the reading of the Ellesmere MS. in l. 418) have the same sense and the same etymology—Latin *regalem* ; but *real* is the early French form, and *roial* is a later borrowing from Parisian French.

413 *as it were a grym leõun* : 'like a fierce lion' ; in fact, the ancients believed that a cock, by his superb bearing, could overawe a lion. Pliny, *Natural History*, x. 21 :— '(superbe) graditur, ardua cervice, cristis celsa; . . . caelumque sola volucrum aspicit crebro; in sublime caudam quoque falcatam erigens; itaque terrori sunt etiam leonibus'.

421–4 An elaborate way of saying 'on May 3rd', on which date, for some obscure reason, Palamon breaks his prison (Knight's Tale A. 1462 f.), and Pandarus persuades Criseyde to hear Troilus's suit (*Troilus* ii, 56). But how is the date deduced from the clumsy expression? Omit *syn Marche bigan* and all is clear, for March = 31 days; 32 days were *also* passed; and 63 days bring us to May 3rd. The insertion of *syn Marche bigan* is easiest explained by a paraphrase:—'When (i) the 31 days of March were passed (*compleet*), and (ii) 32 days in addition to them (= *also*) were passed: then adding (i) and (ii) together, and reckoning *from the first of March*, we get May 3rd.

421 *the monthe in which the world bigan* : from the story of Genesis authoritative writers such as St. Ambrose and Bede assumed that the creation took place about the vernal equinox (March 21st), and Bede, placing three of the six days of Creation before that date, makes March 18th the first day of the world.

428 f. The Zodiac is an imaginary circular band round the heavens, and the sun's annual course is the middle of this band. The band was divided among 12 signs of the Zodiac, the first Aries 'the Ram', the second Taurus 'the Bull', &c., and each of these signs was allotted a twelfth of the circular band, i.e. 30 degrees. As the number of degrees in a circle and the number of days in the year are approximately the same, 1 day is approximately 1 degree of the sun's course round the Zodiac, and 1 month (30 days) is approximately the time the sun would spend in each sign of the Zodiac. The sun was reckoned to begin in the first sign, Aries, on March 12th, which was then, owing to a miscalculation, supposed to be the vernal equinox. Then 11 days of March, *plus* 30 days for the 30 degrees of Aries, *plus* 21 days for the 21 degrees of Taurus traversed, bring us to May 2nd. One day more is accounted for by Chaucer's *somwhat moore*, and an allowance for the error in reckoning 1 degree as 1 day.

433 *fourty degrees and oon and moore* : In l. 428 f. the reckoning applied to the *annual* course of the sun through the signs of the Zodiac, which gives the month and the day. Here the *daily* course of the sun from horizon to horizon is referred to, in order to give the hour of the day. It happens that on May 3rd the sun would have risen just a little over 41 degrees by 9 a. m. (i. e. *pryme*).

438 'a sad mischance befell him'.

439 Cp. the Vulgate, Proverbs xiv. 13 'extrema gaudii luctus occupat'. So Troilus iv. 834 ff.

> Endeth than love in wo? Ye, or men lieth;
> And every worldly joye, as thinketh me:
> The ende of blisse ay sorwe it occupieth!

and Man of Law's Tale 421 ff.

> O sodeyn wo, that ever art súccessòur
> To worldly blisse . . .
> Wo occupieth the fyn of oure gladnesse.

441–3 These lines seem to be rather pointless elaboration. Perhaps they are meant as humorous support to the truth of the story, like ll. 445–7; the argument being:—that woe follows bliss is certain enough to be recorded in a chronicle history; therefore the Cock's mishap, which is an instance of this, is as true as a chronicle.

446 *the book of Launcelot de Lake*: the story of Lancelot, the perfect knight and lover of Arthur's queen, Guinevere. Chaucer refers to the French prose *Lancelot*, or some derivative from it. The early Scottish *Lancelot du Laik*, which has no poetical merit, is about a century later than Chaucer; and the first considerable English version of the Lancelot story is Malory's *Morte d'Arthur* in 1470.

447 *That wommen holde*: ambiguous. *Who* was not yet in use as a relative, so *that* was used both of persons and things. Here *that* probably refers to Lancelot, the ideal knight, rather than to *the book* of Lancelot. Cp. Squire's Tale 287.

448 *torne*: Ellesmere MS. *come*; a good instance of a copyist's error, for in hands of the time *t* and *c* are hard to distinguish, and *rn* is easily misread as *m*. Cp. note to 596.

450 *yeres three*: presumably because it rimes with *iniquitee*.

451 *By heigh ymaginacioun forncast*: 'foreseen by the exalted imagination'—referring to Chantecler's dream. Others take it as 'pre-destined by God'.

452 *the samè nyght*: i. e. in the early hours of the same morning, which were reckoned as part of the night. *hegges*: here apparently in the general sense 'fences', cp. l. 82.

455 *wortes*: probably 'cabbages' as in the *Roman de Renart*, Introd. § ii.

456 *undren*: strictly 9 a.m., but often used loosely, as here, to cover the whole forenoon.

457 *waitynge his tyme*: 'watching his opportunity'. Note how easily the original sense of *wait* (which is a borrowing from Northern French, equivalent to Parisian and modern French *guetter*) merges into the modern sense; and how a new transitive sense of *watch* (< OE. *wæccan* intrans., derived from the same stem *wak-* that is the base of *wait*) develops in the late Middle English and takes the place of *wait* 'to watch'.

461 *Scariot*: Judas Iscariot; for the loss of the initial unaccented vowel cp. *Spain* < French *Espagne* < Latin *Hispania*. *Genyloun*:

Ganelon in the *Roman de Roland*, who betrayed the rear-guard of Charlemagne's army at Roncesvalles. He is the typical traitor of the Charlemagne romances, as Judas is in the Bible, and Sinon in the Troy Romance. It was Sinon who had charge of the horse full of men which was treacherously introduced into Troy, and in the classical version of the story he persuaded Priam to receive it into the city as an offering to Pallas ; *Aeneid* ii. 57 ff.

470 *Witnesse on hym that any parfit clerk is* : 'take any finished scholar as witness (that) ; i. e. ' any good scholar will tell you (that) '.

471 *in scole* : in the schools of philosophy at the Universities.

473 *and hath been of*, &c. : 'and (in the past) there has been discussion by countless men '.

474 *bulte it to the bren* : a metaphor from the sifting or boulting of flour to separate it from the less valuable bran.

475 *Agustyn* : St. Augustine, bishop of Hippo in Africa (354–430), not the apostle of the Anglo-Saxons. In Augustine's time the Welsh scholar Pelagius began the ' Pelagian ' heresy, claiming that man is not necessarily sinful, but has the power, of his own will, to choose between good and evil. To this St. Augustine opposed the doctrine of grace : man is sinful since Adam's fall, and only by the grace of God can he do anything good. This leads to the doctrine that God foreknows and foreordains all things ; and the various attempts to leave some room for human choice are so intricate and so debatable that Chaucer very wisely refuses to meddle with them. The Late Latin form *Agust-* for *August-* is found as early as the first century A. D.

476 *Boece* : Anicius Manlius Severinus Boethius (d. 524) attained consular rank, and was the trusted adviser of the Emperor Theodoric ; but in the end he was put to death by his cruel master. In his last imprisonment he wrote in prose and verse one of the great books of the Middle Ages, the *de Consolatione Philosophiae*, which kept alive the tradition of Aristotle and Plato. King Alfred translated it, so did Chaucer, and Queen Elizabeth after him. It seems to have been Chaucer's favourite book. See notes to 477 ff. and 528.

the Bisshop Bradwardyn : Thomas Bradwardine (d. 1349) distinguished himself by his lectures at Merton College, Oxford, which were put together in a huge book, *de Causa Dei contra Pelagium*. He adopts and develops the position taken up by St. Augustine : that man can only resist temptation by divine grace, which he can never deserve ; and that God's foreknowledge is absolute. He was consecrated Archbishop of Canterbury in 1349, and died in the Great Plague of that year.

477–84 Chaucer states three positions:

(i) ll. 477–9 God foreknows and foreordains all things.

(ii) ll. 480–2 God foreknows, but free choice to do or not to do is left to man.

(iii) ll. 483–4 God foreknows, but his foreknowledge involves not 'simple necessity', but only 'conditional necessity', to do a thing.

He is thinking of the passage at the end of Boethius *de Consolatione Philosophiae*. Philosophy maintains that God foreknows all things and yet that there is room for free-will. Boethius raises the obvious objection—that the one precludes the other. Philosophy replies that the difficulty is due to human failure to conceive of the simplicity of God's nature, and ends a long argument by distinguishing two kinds of necessity : *simple necessity*, e.g. that men should die or the sun rise ; and *conditional necessity*, that a man should take a walk. In the second she claims that there is an element of free-will ; and though God knows that the man will walk, His foreknowledge does not make it necessary that the man should walk. This long and subtle argument, which hardly stills doubt, should be read in Chaucer's translation.

487 *with sorwe* : 'with disastrous results'.

490 *Wommennes conseils*, &c. : a proverb of Norse origin : ON. *köld eru opt kvenna ráð*, lit. 'cold are often women's counsels', where *cold* means 'baneful'. It occurs in the Proverbs of Alfred (thirteenth century): *cold red is quene red*. For a defence of women's counsel, see Tale of Melibeus § 15.

493 *ther as* : 'where' ; cp. note to Monk's Tale 753 above.

494–500 Such apologies are very characteristic of Chaucer, and he usually makes the excuses that he is merely the reporter of somebody else's words and that it is all in fun ; cp. Prologue 724 ff. Their model is *Roman de la Rose* 15159 ff., and particularly the apology to women, 15195 ff., which is followed here.

500 *divyne* : the verb 'divine', 'suppose', which is construed either with *of* or *on* ; see the footnote.

503 *agayn the sonne* : 'in the sun '—'opposite to the sun ' in the sense that she lay full in its rays.

505 *Phisiologus* : A book (or the supposed author of a book) of beasts, birds and precious stones, with marvellous accounts of their nature and properties, and a religious interpretation. It seems to have arisen as a Greek book of instruction in Alexandria, perhaps as early as the second century ; and it was soon translated into Latin and the chief languages of the Near East. From the Latin version came the medieval *Bestiaries*, of which there are Anglo-

Saxon fragments, a full Anglo-Norman version by Philippe de Thaon, and a Middle English version (ed. R. Morris, *An Old English Miscellany*, Early English Text Society). The section on the Fox is a fair sample ; it is his habit to cover himself with red earth, sham death and hang out his tongue : when birds come to eat his tongue he catches them. He signifies the Devil, &c. The Siren sings in rough weather to attract ships, and her sweet voice makes the mariners forget their danger. The Siren signifies Riches ; the Sea the World, &c. In these works the statements are regularly introduced by ' Physiologus says '. Of course Chaucer is laughing at the authority he adduces.

507 f. This picture of Chantecler—his eye led to the cabbages that hide the Fox by the flutterings of an attractive butterfly—rivals any of the touches of nature in the *Roman de Renart*.

510 *Nothyng ne liste hym*: 'he desired not at all'. Cp. note to l. 12.

518 *wher wol ye gon ?*: *wher* is perhaps ' where', perhaps the short form of *whether* used to introduce a direct question : ' Are you going away ?' Cp. note to l. 365.

521 *wolde*: 'purposed'.

522 *youre conseil for t'espye*: ' to spy out your secrets'.

528 *Boéce*: Boethius (cp. note to l. 476). He passed down to the Middle Ages not only the philosophy of the classics, but also much of their science in three treatises : *Institutio Arithmetica*, based on the Greek writer Nicomachus of Gerasa; *Institutio Musica*, based on Nicomachus, Ptolemy, Euclid and other Greek sources; and *Geometria*, a lost work based on Euclid. The second treatise, written in five books, is referred to here.

530 *of hire gentillesse*: ' their' not 'her'.

531 *to my greet ese*: a veiled allusion to their fate.

533 *But for men speke of syngyng*: 'but since singing has been mentioned ', cp. note to l. 624. A polite and not too pointed return to the subject he himself has started.

534 'So may I have good use of my two eyes !'—a common asseveration in Middle English : *brouke* < OE. *brūcan* 'to enjoy'; cp. note to l. 50. But here there is irony in the tag, for the Fox is going on to persuade Chantecler not to use his eyes.

542 *smal*: 'slender', cp. l. 139 n.

546 *daun Burnel the Asse*: another name for the *Speculum Stultorum* or ' Mirror of Fools', a Latin satirical poem written towards the end of the twelfth century by Nigel Wireker, a monk of Christ Church, Canterbury. The Ass, who typifies the monastic order, is its hero, and his name *Burnel* is a variant of *Brunel* (the ' little brown ' animal) which is still used in France as a name for a donkey. The Ass

wants to have a longer tail. His physician Galen tells him that he is as well furnished in this respect as King Louis of France, but gives him a prescription and advises him to go to the famous medical school of Salernum for the drugs. On his way back from Salernum a dog bites off half Burnel's tail, and he loses his medicines; so he decides to go to the University of Paris to become a scholar. On his way to Paris he falls in with a traveller called Arnold, who tells him this story :—Gundulf, the priest's son, when chasing a hen out of the barn, gave one of her chickens a knock with a stick and broke its leg. The time came when the bishop was to ordain Gundulf at a neighbouring town, so that he might succeed his father in the benefice ; but on that morning the injured chicken, which had been nursing its vengeance for five years, refused to crow punctually and waken the candidate. Gundulf, arriving too late, missed the bishop and his ordination, and was ruined for life. The poem is edited by T. Wright in *Anglo-Latin Satirical Poets and Epigrammatists of the Twelfth Century* (Rolls Series, 1872, vol. i), see p. 54.

549 *Whil he was yong and nyce* : i. e. while the priest's son was young and foolish (*nyce*).

551–3 The meaning seems to be 'Certainly there is no comparison between your father's wisdom and judgement and that cock's ingenuity' ; '*of* his subtiltee' is used illogically, as if the old construction *comparisoun of* had preceded, instead of *comparisoun bitwixe*.

555 *Lat se* : 'show me'; lit. 'let ⟨one⟩ see', with ellipse of the indefinite pronoun in the objective.

559–64 *Allas, ye lordes* :—Such an aside may be explained either as Chaucer's comment, or as a mere rhetorical address by the story-teller, made though there were no lords among the pilgrims to profit by it. Either view is possible here. But as the latter explanation is unsatisfactory for the words to 'chanouns religious' in the Canon's Yeoman's Tale l. 992 ff., or to 'ye maistresses that lordes doghtres han in governaunce' in the Doctor's Tale ll. 72 ff., there is no reason to accept it here in order to favour the 'dramatic' view of Chaucer's work. § iv, at the end.

560 Cp. *Legend of Good Women* Prol. 352 :—

For in youre courte ys many a losengeour.

Both are imitated from *Roman de la Rose* 1034 : 'A sa court ot maint losengier '.

563 *Ecclesiaste* : usually refers to Solomon as the author of Ecclesiastes, where there is no appropriate passage. But in the Wife of Bath's Prologue *Ecclesiaste* is applied to Ecclesiasticus,

and it may have the same meaning here : Mr. Pollard compares the Vulgate, Ecclus. xxvii. 26 ' In conspectu oculorum tuorum condulcabit os suum et super sermones tuos admirabitur' etc.   But it may stand for Solomon in any of his works, and refer to Proverbs xxix. 5, which is quoted in Chaucer's Tale of Melibeus in the section on flattery (B. 2368) :—' Salomon seith that " the wordes of a flaterere is a snare to cacche with innocentz "'.   The advice of the flatterer Placebo in the Merchant's Tale, as contrasted with that of the truthful Justinus, illustrates Chaucer's point.

565-7 Chantecler carries out punctually the Fox's suggestions in ll. 539-42, which are very well thought out.

568 *daun Russell* : see Introduction, § iii, p. xxiii.

569 ff. Cp. with what follows *The False Fox*, a poem of the fifteenth century :—

> The fals fox came unto oure croft
> And so oure gese ful fast he sought :
>   With how, fox, how ! with hey, fox, hey !
>   Come no more unto oure house to bere our gese aweye ! . . .
>
> The fals fox came *into oure yerde*,
> And there he made the gese aferde ; &c. . . .
>
> He toke a gose fast *by the nek*
> And the goose thoo began to quek ; &c.
>
> The *good wyfe came out* in her smok
> And at the fox she threw *hir rok* ; &c.
>
> The good man came out with his flayle
> And smote the fox upon the tayle ; &c.
>
> He threw a gose *upon his bak*
> And furth he went thoo with his pak ; &c.
>
> The good man swore, yf that he myght,
> He wolde hym slee or it were nyght ; &c.
>
> The fals fox went into his denne
> And there he was full mery thenne ; &c. . . .
>
> The good man saide unto his wyfe
> ' This fals fox lyveth a mery lyfe ! '
>   With how, fox, how, &c.
>   (*Reliquiae Antiquae* i. p. 4.)

570 Cp. l. 13 of the poem just quoted ; and ll. 613, 639, below.

572 *O Destinee* ! From here to l. 607 the mock heroics are rather overdone.

581 *O Gaufred* : about the end of the twelfth century Geoffrey de Vinsauf, an Englishman who spent a good deal of time at Rome, wrote his *Nova Poetria*, a manual for poets containing precepts, with some examples of Geoffrey's own composition. Hence Chaucer calls him ironically *deerë maister sovèrayn*. Among the examples is a lament for the death of Richard I, who received his mortal wound from an arrow on Friday, March 26, 1199, though he lingered on till April 6. It runs:

> O Veneris lacrimosa dies ! O sidus amarum !
> Illa dies tua nox fuit, et Venus illa venenum !
> Illa dedit vulnus, &c.

The most accessible account of Geoffrey and his work is in Thomas Wright's *Biographia Britannica Literaria* (Anglo-Norman Period), pp. 398 ff.

575 f. *Friday* : i.e. the day of Venus, Latin *dies Veneris*, OE. *Frīgedæg*, because the goddess Frīg was identified with Venus. Remember, too, that the sun was in Taurus, the ' house ' of Venus.

584 *ne hadde I* : two syllables, the scansion being the same as for the contracted form *nadde I*. It might be better to read *nadde* here, for in l. 303 the different scansion shows that there is no contraction. *Sentence* = 'noble sentiments'.

585 *as diden ye* : Chaucer changes from the singular to the plural pronoun when it suits his rime. Generally the singular is used to address a divinity (e. g. 285, 576), a familiar or an inferior; the plural in polite and formal speech, as in ll. 1–39, 142-203. But there is a certain amount of crossing, e. g. *maistow* 340; *thee* 342, compared with *ye, yow* 355 f. ; and too much should not be made of the distinction.

590 *Ylioun,* or *Ilium* : Troy, or perhaps its citadel. In *Hous of Fame* 151 ff. Chaucer sees depicted on the walls of the temple of glass the destruction of Troy—Sinon and the horse, the assault of Ilium, and the slaying of Priam by Pyrrhus. In both passages he follows the *Aeneid*, not the medieval version of the story found in Guido de Columnis, which is different in many details.

591 f. *Pirrus with his streitè swerd Whan he*, &c.

(i) *Pirrus . . . whan he* is a clumsy expression for *Whan Pirrus . . .* (ii) *streitè* seems to reflect Latin *stricta (acie)*, but the words do not occur in *Aeneid* ii, 468 ff. where the slaying of Priam by Pyrrhus is described, though they are found at l. 334 of the same book. Guido de Columnis has *ense nudo.* (iii) In Virgil, Pyrrhus seized Priam by the hair—*implicuitque coma laevam*—not by the beard. There is nothing similar in Guido.

593 *Eneydos* : the Greek genitive with *liber* understood. Near the beginning of the Monk's Tale we have ' as *Judicum* can telle' where *Judicum* stands for *liber Judicum* ' the book of Judges '. Scan *E/ne/y/dos* (four syllables).

596 *sovèreynly* : the Ellesmere MS. reads *sodevnly*, an obvious error of the copyist ; for *d* in MSS. of the time is formed something like Greek δ, and *ver* is represented by *v* (or *u*) with a hook above it as a contraction for *er*. The two words are thus almost identical in script. Cp. note to 448.

597 ff. *Hasdrubales wyf* : this Hasdrubal was not the brother of Hannibal (d. B.C. 207), but the Carthaginian leader whom Scipio Africanus Minor defeated in B.C. 146. After a desperate resistance Hasdrubal gave himself up to save his life, and, indignant at his weakness, his wife threw herself and her sons into the flames. Chaucer reads her motive differently ; cp. Franklin's Tale (F. 1399 ff.) :

> What shal I seyn of Hasdrubales wyf
> That at Cartáge birafte hirself hir lyf ?
> For whan she saugh that Romayns wan the toun,
> She took hir children alle and skipte adoun
> Into the fyr, and chees rather to dye
> Than any Romayn dide hire vileynye.

His source is Jerome's *contra Iovinianum*. bk. i, a treatise written about the year 392 in answer to the heretic Jovinian, who argued that widows and wives were as meritorious as virgins. Jerome's treatise is referred to by the Wife of Bath (D. 674 f.) in a passage which may well describe a book in Chaucer's own library. It certainly was a favourite of his.

600 *She* : Hasdrubal's wife, not Pertelote.

604 f. *Nero* : Again one of the stories used by the Monk is mentioned without any backward reference (cp. l. 372 f. and note) :

> He Romè brende for his delicasie ;
> The senatours he slow upon a day
> To heeren how men woldè wepe and crie.

Both passages are probably inspired by Boethius, bk. ii, metre 6 : ' he leet brennen the cité of Rome, and made sleen the senatours '.

613 *and bar* : the preterite *bar* ' bore ' is not logical here : modern English also would avoid the logical sequence with the present infinitive *and bere*, preferring the present participle ' bearing '.

617 *Colle* ... *Talbot* ... *Gerland* : *Colle* seems to have been a common name for a dog, and a diminutive of it may be the origin of *collie*. But it is also applied to persons, usually of low station, e. g. Colle the juggler in *Hous of Fame* 1277. *Talbot* and *Gerland* belong to the hunting tradition, for hounds were given very dis-

tinguished names ; cp. the short list in the Introduction, p. xxi ; and the very elaborate list in *Roman de Renart*, Branch v, 1187 ff. *Talbot* as a hound's name occurs in a fifteenth-century hunting song printed by Chambers and Sidgwick, *Early English Lyrics*, p. 245. *Gerland* is probably the Breton name of which Grelant is another form—not our word 'garland'.

618 *Malkyn*: a diminutive of *Matilda*, commonly used for a serving-maid. The distaff appears regularly in the chase of the Fox ; it is the *rok* of 'The False Fox' quoted in the note to l. 569 ff.

620 *Sóre aferd for berkyng of the dogges*: i. e. 'because of the barking'. The readings of the eight printed MSS. are :

(i) *for berkyng of the dogges* Ellesmere, Hengwrt, Corpus, Lansdowne ; *for berkyng of dogges* Harley 7334, Petworth ; *for the berkyng of the dogges* Cambridge Gg and Dd. The weight of evidence supports the first reading, and the others may be set aside as attempts to mend the metre.

(ii) *sore aferd* Corpus, Lansdowne, Petworth ; *so fered* Ellesmere, Hengwrt, Cambridge Dd ; *for-fered* Cambridge Gg ; *so were they fered* Harley 7334 (so Skeat, Pollard). *for-fered* may be rejected at once as bad idiom. The two groups, headed by Corpus and Ellesmere, and generally admitted to be independent witnesses in some degree, are here divided. But whereas the Ellesmere reading makes bad metre and doubtful idiom (the best defence would be to take it closely with l. 622, supplying *that*), the Corpus reading makes good metre and good idiom, for *sore aferd (of)* occurs in the Knight's Tale (A. 1518) and *Legend of Good Women* Prol. A. 53. It remains to consider the reading of Harley 7334, a very erratic MS.: it is clumsily phrased, makes a bad rhythm with the best established text of the rest of the line, and is pretty clearly a patching of *so fered*. I assume that the original reading was *sore aferd* ; that it was miscopied *so ferd*, and that all the other readings are attempts to mend the construction or the metre.

622 'it seemed to them that their hearts broke'—*breek* is preterite.

624 *as men wolde hem quelle*: 'as if they were being killed'—*men* is impersonal and best translated by the passive.

627 *a benedicitee* ; 'O bless us !' a very common exclamation ; *benedicite* is regularly scanned as three syllables, except in the Knight's Tale A. 1785 : The god of love, *a benedicitee*. The spelling *bendistee* is sometimes found in MSS., and gives the usual pronunciation.

628 *he Jakkè Straw*: a construction natural enough in conversation, and very common in Chaucer. Thus within fifty lines (E. 1692 ff.) of the Merchant's Tale we have : *That she this*

mayden . . .; Nor he Theodamus . . .; the wedding *of hire Philologie and hym Mercurie.*

Jack Straw was one of the leaders of the Peasants' Revolt in 1381, and he seems to have struck the imagination of contemporaries more than his colleague Wat Tyler did. The rebels planned a concentration on London, and their main forces were encamped on Blackheath by June 12th of that year. They began negotiations with the King's government to secure their aims, which were, in general, freedom from oppressive laws, customs and taxes. A strong party among the citizens favoured the rebels, and when the peasants entered the city, the jealousy of the London workmen and apprentices directed their attacks against foreigners, whose prosperity was their chief offence. The Flemings had been encouraged by Edward III, and they were principally concerned in the woollen trade as manufacturers, merchants and skilled artisans. They were ruthlessly beheaded by the mobs, who are said to have used the shibboleth 'bread & cheese' which Flemings called 'brode and kase'. The uproar was so hideous that it seems to have impressed all observers. June 14 was the chief day of the massacres. On the 15th Walworth the Mayor struck down Wat Tyler at Smithfield, and from that moment the vengeance of authority on the rebels began. According to Froissart Jack Straw and the priest John Ball ' were found in an old house hidden, thinking to have stolen away, but they could not, for they were accused by their own men. Of the taking of them the King and his lords were glad, and they strake off their heads, and Wat Tyler's also, and they were set on London Bridge.' Jack Straw's confession is reported by Walsingham *Historia Anglicana* (Rolls Series) ii, 9–10. So for a few days he flashes in and out of history. Two poems referring to him are in T. Wright's *Political Poems and Songs* (Rolls Series) i. 224 ff. For narratives of the Revolt, and the contemporary authorities, see *Le Soulèvement des Travailleurs d'Angleterre en 1381,* by A. Réville and C. Petit-Dutaillis, Paris 1898 ; and Oman *The Great Revolt of 1381,* Oxford 1906.

632 *box :* wood of the box-tree.

634 *skriked :* the variant *shriked* is perhaps the better reading, because Chaucer elsewhere has only *shrighte* &c. For some unexplained reason the OE. initial group *scr-* seems to yield ME. forms with *shr-* (which is the normal development) and with *skr-* ; and here some MSS. have one and some the other. Note that the alternative form *shrighte* (l. 596) would not fill the verse.

641 *if that I were as ye :* 'if I were in your place ', 'if I were you '.

642 *as wys God helpe me !* a regular form of asseveration, 'as

sure (*wys*) as God may help me !': or it may be paraphrased
' truly, so help me God !'

652 *y-gon*: the best MSS. have *gon*; *igon* is the reading of
Harley 7334; *agon* would be in accord with Chaucer's usage,
cp. l. 264. Not to be explained as omission of a syllable after
the caesura, because here there is no pause.

664 *do me to synge*: ' cause me to sing'.

673 ff. Cp. with these lines the Preamble to the Parson's Tale,
where the Host asks for a fable:

> This Persoune answerede al at ones
> 'Thou getest fable noon y-toold for me,
> For Poul, that writeth unto Thymothee,
> Repreveth hem that weyveth soothfastnesse,
> And tellen fables and swich wrecchednesse.
> Why sholde I sowen draf out of my fist
> Whan I may sowen whete, if that me list?
> For which I seye, if that yow list to heere
> Moralitee and vertuous mateere, &c.

Having told a fable, the Nun's Priest anticipates this very objection,
and ingeniously quotes St. Paul, the same authority that the Parson
quotes in the opposite sense!

673 *As of a fox*: here *as* is best interpreted according to the
note to l. 102, and left out of account in construing.

675 *Seint Poul seith*: Romans xv. 4: Quaecumque enim scripta
sunt, ad nostram doctrinam scripta sunt. The quotation in its
context is hardly so sweeping. In the Retracciouns at the end of
the Canterbury Tales, Chaucer writes: ' and if ther be anythyng that
displese hem, I preye hem also that they arrette (*impute*) it to the
defaute of myn unkonnynge, and nat to my wyl ... for oure boke
seith " Al that is writen is writen for oure doctrine", and that is
myn entente '

On the forme *Poul*, see note to l. 14. The Ellesmere MS. has
Paul here, and there is evidence elsewhere in Chaucer MSS. that
the Latinized form was coming into use in citations from Scripture.

679 *As seith my lord*: a crux, which I cannot solve. What
follows is simply discussion.

(i) On the general effect of ll. 678–80, note that Middle English
secular compositions—*Havelok* for instance or *Sir Gawain*—
usually close with a prayer, whether for the audience or the reciter
or the composer. The practice is probably borrowed from sermons,
in which it is established from an early date; in any event, it is
inspired by the same spirit.

(ii) Chaucer follows the old tradition, so that a prayer is the normal ending of a completed tale, whatever may be the character of the story or its narrator. Three points are worth noting:— (1) The prayers at the end of the first three tales (Knight, Miller, Reeve) have a general likeness, as against all the rest. Perhaps these three tales were written, or were revised for inclusion in the Canterbury Tales, at about the same time. (2) The serious lines which appear so abruptly in the Pardoner's Tale (C. 916-8) are of this nature, making the true close of his sermon. Professor Kittredge's interpretation of them as the expression of a sudden emotional crisis (*Chaucer and his Poetry*, p. 216 f.) does not take account of their formal purpose; though that purpose is consistent with sincerity. (3) The Parson's Tale has no such ending. But Chaucer's Retracciouns at the end of it spring from the same mood and the same tradition: they are the prayer for the author which naturally closes the whole work, and cannot be considered as an excrescence, still less as a last jape of the poet or as a forgery.

(iii) The ending of Chaucer's *A, B, C*, will help to distinguish general phrases from those that may be special to the Nun's Priest's Tale:

> Now, Lady brihtè, *sith thou canst and wilt*
> Ben to the sede of Adam merciable,
> *So bring us* to that palais that is bilt
> To penitents that ben to mercy able.

Here the first line is parallel to l. 679 (for it could be asserted of the Virgin Mary that she could and would help by intercession); the third and fourth cover l. 680, and show that *so* is not a correlative to *as*, but the polite imperative (cp. note to l. 177). In *Troilus* v, 1868 *So make us, Jesus, for thy mercy digne*, we get the equivalent of l. 679 without the crux. But *As seith my lord* is not comparable with anything in other endings. *As seith* (*St. Poul*, &c.) is the regular way of introducing a citation from authority; and since Chaucer always uses *oure Lord* = 'Jesus', *my lord* should refer to a lord in this world.

(iv) There is no real difficulty in the transition from *Now goodè God* 679 to *his heighè blisse* 680, for in a prayer to God, the confusion between direct address and address in the third person is natural enough.

(v) The Ellesmere and other MSS. contain a certain number of marginal explanatory notes, which are on the whole well-informed. Often they give references to Latin sources used, and quote the Latin in a form nearer to Chaucer's English than any known text is. Occasionally they are wrong or pointless, like the entry *Petrus Comestor* (the author of the twelfth-century *Historia Scholastica*) at l. 443 of our text. Opposite *as seith my lord* appears the note:

59

scilicet Dominus archiepiscopus Cantuariensis.   Is this Chaucer's own explanation? Probably not, for no greater acumen than the earliest editors of Chaucer had, is required to guess a reference to the archbishop in the use of *my lord* by a priest on a Canterbury pilgrimage who could hardly have any other lord.   Besides, it bears the stamp of the commentator's art, for while it seems to bring light, it really explains nothing : why should the archbishop be referred to here? It has been suggested that the archbishop of the time (William Courtenay 1381-96) may have had the absurd habit of qualifying every prayer with *if be thy wille* ; but the parallel quoted above from the *A, B, C* must be reckoned with ; the phrase is a common one usually meaning little more than ' please ' ; and even if it has a full sense, in the days when predestination and salvation by grace were orthodox doctrine (cp. note to l. 476), there would be nothing absurd in the prayer ' Make us all good, if it be Thy will '.

Other lines of solution are not successful.   The prayer ' Make us all good men ' seems to have no liturgical use which would associate it with the archbishop ; and it is hardly satisfactory to assume that the Nun's Priest, feeling the need of some authority higher than his own to bless the company, uses the regular phrase for introducing an acknowledged authority, with words which the archbishop, as the head of the English Church, might say at the end of a sermon.

To sum up, if the marginal note is right, we do not know why the archbishop is referred to.   If the note is wrong, *as seith my lord* is possibly a remnant of some use of the story in a different setting, without which the meaning is irrecoverable.

EPILOGUE : see note to l. 43 above.

CHAUCER'S ENGLISH

§ 1. **Changes of Meaning.**—The number of words in the Nun's Priest's Tale which have no representatives in Modern English is not really great—perhaps some fifty in all, and of these a few, e. g. *bewray, hent, shent, maugree*, are known as literary archaisms. The real difficulty lies not in them, but in many changes of meaning. Some are obvious enough, e. g. *catel* 'property' (not 'cattle') 61 n., *rente* 'revenues coming in' (not 'rent', which is an out-going payment for land, houses, &c.) 61 n., *sentence* 'opinions', &c. 211, *departen* 'part' 227, *casuelly* 'by accident' 335, *stynte* 'stop' (not 'stint') 391 ; and others are more troublesome because they are not so obvious. Any one who is content to render *his snowtĕ smal* 139, by 'his small snout', or *rome* 132, 414, by 'roam', or *pasture* 419 by 'pasture', is reading an imperfectly modernized version of Chaucer, for *small*, which once meant, 'slim', &c., has become more general in its meaning ; *roam* has acquired a sense of spaciousness which forbids us to talk of a person roaming in a small chamber ; and *pasture* then meant not only 'grass-land' or 'grass', but anything that is eaten, and the act of feeding itself. A reader who is constantly on the alert, and tries to give a precise meaning to each word or phrase, will find a new pleasure in Chaucer.

§ 2. **Dialect.**—Chaucer lived in London, and wrote in the East Midland dialect of London, which by his time was becoming the literary language of England. Hence his work is much easier to read than contemporary poems in other dialects, such as *Sir Gawain and the Green Knight, Pearl*, or *Piers Plowman*.

Note. It is important to examine the rimes, because scribes cannot easily alter them without being detected. They show a certain number of forms proper to the Kentish dialect, which extended westward as far as London. Thus an Anglo-Saxon etymological *y* became *i* in Northern Middle English, and in most of the Midlands ; in the western districts of the South and Midlands it often appears as *u* ; in Kentish it became *e*. Hence from Anglo-Saxon *myrige* we have normal Midland *mirie, myrie,*

51, 305; West Midland *murie* 49, 85; and Kentish *mery* (in rime) 200. Here, exceptionally, modern English has standardized the Kentish form, instead of *mirry*. Again OE. *styntan* gives East Midland *stinte* and Kentish *stente* : the first appears at l. 391, the second in M.T. 745 (riming with *sente*) ; OE. *lystan* gives East Midland *liste* 510 and Kentish *leste* (riming with *reste*) 307. *Sterte* 601 (riming with *herte*) beside *stirten* 611, is probably to be explained in the same way. *Keen* 'kine' 65 (OE. *cȳ* pl.), is another Kentish form ; see Glossary.

§ 3. **Spelling and Pronunciation.**—Chaucer's spelling would seem less strange if we were accustomed to read sixteenth- and seventeenth-century texts in their original form instead of in modernized editions. The spelling of a good MS. like the Ellesmere is fairly consistent, and roughly phonetic in the sense that a letter usually has some sound-value. Note that (1) *k* often stands for modern hard *c*, e. g. *kan, koude.* (2) *-aun-* is usual for modern *-an-* in borrowings from French, e. g. *daunce* 74, *Chauntecleer* 83, *governaunce* 99, where *-aun-* represented the sound which we still have in *launch, vaunt.* (3) *i* and *y* are equivalent, cp. *malencolie* 167 and *malencolye* 180 ; but *y* is preferred in the neighbourhood of *u, m, n,* which are easily confused with *i* in script : hence regular *his* but *hym, right* but *nyght.* (4) *ou* and *ow* are alternatives, e. g. *lowde* 15, *loude* 540. (5) So are *-ey-* (*-ei-*), *-ay-* (*-ai-*), e. g. *pray* 27, *prey* 636 ; *sovereyn* 443, *soverayn* 581. (6) The long vowels *ē, ā, ō* are often doubled : *somdeel* 55, *wheer* 133, *heele* 184 ; *estaat* 9, *taak* 177, *maad* 590 ; *moore* 'more' 1, *foond* (OE. *fánd*) 63, *oold* 107.

Note. In *jeet* 'jet' 95, *reed* 'red' 136, *noon* 'none' 151, *oon* 218, *hoot* 'hot' 191, *soond* 'sand' 501, *soong* 'sang' 504, the long vowel has since been replaced by a short.

(i) **Syllables.**—Words have been shortened since Chaucer's day. He could not rime *go : growe*, because the infinitive *gro|wé* would be two syllables (see § 4 below) ; and his verse shows that the inflexions *-ed, -es* were normally syllabic (except in some long words), e. g. *hert|es* 45, *blam|ed* 51. Notice that the suffix *-ioun* makes two syllables, e. g. *a|vys|i|oun, con|clus|i|oun* ; and similarly *pa|ci|ence* 60, *e|quy|nox|i|al* 90.

(ii) **Consonants.**—There are no silent consonant symbols, except initial *h* in French words like *habundant* 159, where it does not prevent elision. *Knyght* and *nyght, wroghte* and *roghte, wlat-som* and *lat,* have distinct initial sounds. *Lyte* 'little' 166 rimes with *bite,* but could not rime with *might* because *gh* had still something of the sound heard in German *ich* or Scots *loch.* In all positions *r* is sounded, e. g. in *rather, mordrour.*

Language

(iii) **Vowels.**—The best rough rule is to follow the Continental pronunciation of Latin :—

(*a*) Short *a, e, i, o, u* are pronounced as in French *patte*, English *pet, pit, pot, put*.

Note. Short *u* is regularly spelt *o* when it occurs alongside *m, n, i, u* (= *v*), which in script are hard to distinguish from *u* (see the facsimile at p. 24). Hence *som* (OE. *sum*); *sone* (OE. *sunu* 'son'); *love* (OE. *lufu*); *above* (OE. *abufan*); *woned* (OE. *wunad* 'dwelt'). Sometimes *o* is found in other positions, e.g. *boter-flye* (OE. *buttor-*) 24.

(*b*) Long *ā, ī, ū* are pronounced as in *father, police, rude*.

Note: Long *ū* is always spelt *ou* (*ow*) according to an Old French practice, e.g. *lowde, bour, broun, bacoun*.

Long *ē* and *ō* have both open and close sounds, which are usually distinguished in the rimes. Close *ẹ̄* was pronounced as in French 'été', open *ẹ̄* as in English 'air'; close *ọ̄* as in French 'eau', open *ọ̄* as in English 'oar'. The distinction of open and close sounds in Chaucer is often difficult.

Note: Long close *ẹ̄* is sometimes distinguished by the spelling *ie*, e.g. *lief* 113 (but *levere* 354). The modern spelling *ea* indicates that the word had open *ẹ̄* in Chaucer's time, e.g. in *great, meal, beat* (ME. *greet, meel, bete*); while modern *ee* usually represents the close vowel, e.g. in *deep, feel, feet*. So modern *oo* indicates ME. close *ọ̄*, e.g. in *sooty, sooth*.

(iv) **Accentuation.**—In words of native origin the incidence of the stress accent is usually the same as in modern English. But words borrowed from French were in a transitional stage. In French the last stem-syllable of nouns is stressed rather more than the others, whereas in English nouns the first syllable carries a strong stress and the later syllables are relatively weak. Ultimately most borrowings from French followed the English rule, but in Chaucer they often retain their original accent, e.g. *solás, cotáge, colóur, corál, prisóun*. Occasionally the English method of accentuation is tried where it has not been maintained, e.g. *révers* 211, modern *revérse*. Sometimes Chaucer takes advantage of the uncertainty to use the form that best suits his metre, e.g. *senténce* 36, but *séntence* 584 ; *ministres* 292, but *ministres* 277 ; and so with the old Norse compound *feláwes* 260, but *féláwe* 264. In polysyllables like *súffisàunce* 73, *áventùre* 233, it is difficult to say whether the first syllable or the third has the stronger stress.

Note. In English words like *hevynèsse* 3, *dawenỳnge* 116, the rimes indicate a secondary stress on the suffix. We should expect *-ness* and *-ing-* to be stronger in Chaucer than in modern English, because they are followed by a weak syllable *-e*, which gives contrast.

§ 4. **Inflexions.**—For the most part the inflexions in Chaucer are similar to those of early modern English as they are recorded in the Prayer Book and the Authorized Version of 1611.

Final -e. But whereas in the fifteenth and sixteenth centuries final -e is added or omitted almost at random by scribes and printers, in Chaucer's English it usually has a grammatical value and is pronounced as a distinct syllable. It represents an Old English unaccented vowel, whether final (as -a, -e, -o, -u) or followed in OE. by flexional -n, -m (as -an, -en, -on, -um) ; and it also represents Old French final -e.

Its commoner uses in inflexion are :—

(i) In the plural of all adjectives (except polysyllables), e. g. *rede lemes* 164, *blaké beres* 169.

(ii) In the singular of weak adjectives (see § 6 below), e. g. *the greté superfluytee* 161 n.

(iii) In various verbal inflexions, particularly
    (*a*) in the infinitive, e. g. *to pleyé* 40, *gladé* 45.
    (*b*) in the 1st sing. pres. indicative, e. g. *tellé* 58.
    (*c*) in the plural pres. indicative, e. g. *syngé* 435, *spryngé* 436.
    (*d*) in the weak pa. t. sing. & pl., e. g. *wenté* 219, 381.
    (*e*) in the strong pa. t. pl., e. g. *ronné* 622.
    (*f*) in the subjunctive, e.g. *helpé* 642.
    (*g*) in the strong past participle, e. g. *understondé* 114.

Note. In (*a*), (*c*), (*e*), (*g*) and the plurals under (*d*), -en is found as well as -e, e.g. *heeren* 7, *desiren* 147, *flowen* 625, *faren* 113, *herden* 610. Normally -e is used before a word beginning with a consonant, and -en before a word beginning with a vowel ; but Chaucer uses the forms for metrical convenience, e.g. *gronen in* (three syllables) 120, but *grone in* (two syllables) 124. So at l. 266 *fallen in* has the variant reading *fallé in gret* with the same number of syllables.

(iv) As the ending of many adverbs, e. g. *sooré* 121, *newé* 283, *fasté* 321, *loudé* 567.

In the fifteenth century final -e was no longer regularly pronounced in the London dialect. The extant Chaucer manuscripts, which date from this time, do not always preserve it correctly ; and early imitators like Lydgate and Hoccleve show by their broken rhythms that they did not understand this secret of his metre. Dryden and Pope were in the same case, and it was not till Tyrwhitt's great edition of 1775-8 that the importance of final -e was realized.

Language

§ 5. Nouns.—The regular endings are :—

	Singular.	Plural.
Nom. Acc.	—	*-es.*
Gen.	*-es.*	*-es.*
Dat.	*-(e).*	*-es.*

Note. (*a*) *-es* is a separate syllable as a rule, except in some longer words, e.g. *messedayes* 86, *husbondes* 606 (but *housbondes* 148 is three syllables).

(*b*) Some borrowings from French make the plural in *-s*, e.g. *paramours* 101, *colours* 102, *replecciouns* 157 ; cp. the variant to *senatoures* 605 (footnote). Note also the plural *vers* ' verses ' 547.

(*c*) *-is* appears for *-es* in *eeris*, *heeris* 137 f., and the rime *beryis* : *mery is* 199 f. indicates that the pronunciation was not very different from that in modern *hors-es* (pronounced *-iz*).

(*d*) *eyen* 139, 395, 539, &c. (OE. pl. *ēagan*) and *toon* 96 in rime (OE. pl. *tān*) retain an old plural ending, which is extended by analogy to *doghtren* 63 (OE. pl. *dohtru* or *dohtor*). But *toos* 565 (in rime) and *doghtres* 609 also occur. On *keen* ' kine ' 65 see Glossary and § 2 above.

(*e*) *-e* often appears in spelling as the ending of the dative singular, but it is not often sounded, and it is hard to be sure that it had not crept into the nominative by analogy. A clear instance is *in londe* 113 riming with pp. *understondé*.

(*f*) Survivals are the gen. sg. *fader* 202 (OE. gen. sg. *fæder*), and the uninflected plural of some nouns with long stems in Old English, e.g. *seven yeer oold* 351 (OE. pl. *gēar* neuter), seven nyght *oold* 107 (OE. pl. *niht* fem.).

§ 6. Adjectives.—The adjective, which was to lose all trace of inflexion in the course of the fifteenth century, is still declined in Chaucer.

(i) The plural of adjectives ends in *-e*, which makes a syllable, e. g. *redé lemes* 164, *ensamples oldé* 340.

(ii) The singular of adjectives ends in *-é* when they follow the weak declension, e. g. *the brighté sonné* 112, *youre redé colera* 162, *Now, goodé God* 678.

Note. (*a*) The weak form of the adjective is used chiefly after demonstratives like *the, this, his, youre* ; and in the vocative.

(*b*) Polysyllables usually have no inflexion, e. g. *fortunat* 10.

(*c*) Note the shortening of the stem vowel in comparison : *whitter* 97, *gretteste* 218.

(*d*) The adjective is postponed, under French influence, in *lif present* 215.

§ 7. Pronouns.

(i) 3rd PERSON.—The personal pronoun of the third person is in the plural Nom. *they*, Poss. *hir(e)*, Obj. *hem*. Thus of the three forms that English borrowed from Norse (*they, their, them*), only the first had been adopted in the London dialect up to the end of the fourteenth century.

Note. (*a*) The possessive pl. *hir(e)* ' their ' 530, 606, is in form the same as the fem. sing. poss. & obj. *hir(e)* 61, 68, 71, 502.

(*b*) *his* is the possessive of *it*, as well as of *he*, e. g. ' the sonne in *his* ascencioun ' 190 ; and *his* is spelt with final -*e* (never pronounced) when it is a plural, e. g. l. 137. Perhaps *his toon* 96 should be corrected.

(ii) 2nd PERSON.—The singular pronouns *thow, thee,* are still used in familiar talk (e. g. ll. 324–31), or in addressing God, e. g. 284 f. The polite plurals *ye, yow* are preferred in more formal language, e. g. l. 2, or when an inferior addresses his superior, e. g. l. 264. But there is a border line in which the distinction is not strictly observed ; see note to l. 585. *Yow* obj. is not confused with *ye* nom. ; see ll. 179-203.

(iii) RELATIVE.—**That** is the usual relative, e. g. *by hevene-kyng* that *for us alle dyde* 30, *two men* that *wolde* 301.

Which sg., *whiche* pl., is also used, both of persons, e. g. 58, and of things, e. g. 67 and perhaps 101. It is also found combined with *that,* e. g. *Catoun* which that *was* 174, or preceded by *the: herbes* . . . The whiche *han* 186.

Who is not used as a relative in Chaucer, but the oblique cases *whos* and *whom* are so used throughout Middle English.

§ 8. Verbs.—

(i) THE PRESENT INDICATIVE.

Singular.	Plural.
i(ch) com-e	*we com-e(n)*
thou com-(e)st	*ye com-e(n)*
he com-(e)th	*they com-e(n)*

Note. (*a*) The plural -*e(n)* is the characteristic inflexion of the Midland dialect (Southern dialects have -(*e*)*th*, Northern -(*e*)*s*). *e(n)* is proved for the original by the rimes at ll. 85 f. (see the note) and 281 f. On the use of -*en* or *e* see § 4 note, above.

(*b*) (*e*)*th* is proved for the original by rimes like *feith : seith* 145 f. The modern ending of the third person singular in -(*e*)*s* had not yet reached the London dialect from the North.

(ii) THE IMPERATIVE PLURAL, which may be used politely where a single person is addressed, ends in -*eth* or -*e*, e. g. *truste* 258, *Herkneth* . . . *And se* 435 f.

(iii) THE PAST TENSE of strong verbs sometimes shows distinctions between singular and plural stems which are now lost, e. g.

sg. *fond* 269, *foond* 63 (OE. *fánd*), but pl. *founde* 282. But Chaucer uses both *they ronné* (the true plural form) 622 and *they ran* 615 (in rime, the true singular form) as it suits his convenience. So in the preterite-present *shal* the plural is usually *shul* (OE. *sculen*), but the true singular form *shal* is also used in the plural *ye shal* 181. Conversely he uses besides the true pa. t. sg. *bar* (OE. *bær*) 613 and *brak* (OE. *bræc*) 650, the sg. forms *beer* 570 and *breek* 622, which take their vowels from the plurals, OE. *bǣron*, *brǣcon*.

(iv) THE PAST PARTICIPLE often retains its old prefix *y-* (OE. *ge-*), though Gower, who was Chaucer's contemporary and friend, avoids this form altogether. Examples are *y-seyled* 333, *y-ronne* 428. In strong verbs the pp. ends in *-(e)n* or *-e*, e. g. *understonde* 114, *founden* 212, *slawe* 248, *slayn* 256, *y-founde* 416, *y-doon* 654, *writen* 675, *y-write* 676.

The remaining verbal forms present little difficulty, and their subsequent history is comprised in the loss of inflexional *-e*, *-en*; the loss of distinctive forms of the 2nd person singular; and the loss of the subjunctive.

§ 9. **Syntax.**—It is impossible to give a brief survey of Chaucer's syntax, and special constructions have therefore been explained in the notes. But, in general, the syntax of literary English has become more and more logical and rigid under classical influences, whereas Chaucer still retains much of the freedom of conversation.

NOTE ON THE METRE

In this tale Chaucer uses a metre that is not found in English before his time—the rimed couplet in which the typical line has five stresses. He seems to have borrowed the rhythm from Italian models like Dante and Boccaccio, and to have realized at once its advantages over the couplet of four-stressed lines which is usual in Old French poets and their English imitators of the fourteenth century.

If stressed syllables are represented by $\_{'}$, and unstressed by $\times$, the normal line is

$$\times \_{'} \mid \times \_{'} \mid \times \_{'} \mid \times \_{'} \mid \times \_{'} (\times)$$

e. g.   Is ríght | ynóugh | to múch|ė fólk | I géss-ė 4
            Hir bórd | was sérv|ed móost | with whít | and blák 77

(1) That final *-e* at the line end (as in *gessé*) makes a syllable is proved by the grammar, and by such rimes as *Romė : to me* Prol. 671 f.; *yowthe : alow the* (= thee) F. 675 f.; *time : by me* G. 1204 f.

(2) Most of the devices used in later poetry to avoid monotony are to be found in Chaucer, e. g. inverted stress in

         Cómth of | the grét|ė sú|perflú|ytée 161 ;

substitution of weak syllables for strong in

         That shul | been for | yourė héelė | and for | yourė prów 184 ;

substitution of secondary accents (here represented by `) for unaccented syllables in

         Mílk and | bróun brèed | in whích | she fóond | no lák 78 ;

and trisyllabic feet in

         Pékkė hem ùp | ríght as | they grówė | and étė | hem ýn 201

or

         And in | this cártė | héerė he lìth | gápyng | upríght 276.

(3) One licence—the omission of the first stress so that the line seems to be a syllable short—is disconcerting to a modern reader, e. g.

         Or | an á|gu that | may be | yourė bán-ė 194
         Sórė | aférd | for bérk|yng of | the dóggės 620
         Ták|eth the | morál|ité | goódė mèn 674.

Note. In ll. 162, 553 the difficulty is avoided if final *-e* of *youre* is made syllabic ; but it is usually silent, and the point requires more investigation. In l. 548 *that* may have been added in the Ellesmere MS. to mend the metre.

Note on the Metre

(4) Élision of final -*e* is indicated in the above examples by a dot under the elided -*ę*. It occurs before a following vowel or a weak *h*; cp.

A póv|rè wýd|wé sóm|deel stápę | ín ág-è 55
This wýd|wę of whích | I téll|é yow | my tál-è 58

Note too—*also͜ of* 17, *she͜ and* 64, *to͜ habundant* 159, *the͜ A|-vis|i|oun* 357, *the͜ oldé* 362, *t'espye* 522, *suffre͜ hym* 580.

(5) Words containing *e* + a liquid or nasal in the second syllable, e. g. *nevere, evere, siker, swevene, seven, hevene, owene* ('own') are usually treated as *nevre, swevne, sevn,* &c. Cp. the scansion of *seven(e)* in ll. 100, 107, 351; and note *colere and* (2 sylls.) 180, *siker as* (2 sylls.) 397; *never erst* (2 sylls.) 515. Words like *symple, cronycle* often make a syllable less than we should expect, e. g. in ll. 442, 479.

(6) On number of syllables see Chaucer's Language, § 3, (i) above, and note *Ma|cro|be|us* 357, *Dan|i|el* 362, *E|ne|y|dos* 593.

(7) On accentuation, see ibid., §. 3, (iv).

(8) On variant forms used for metrical convenience, see note to l. 318 f., and Chaucer's Language § 3, (iv); § 4 note; § 5, note (d); § 8, (iii) and (iv).

(9) The MSS. usually mark a pause within the line, but it is not essential. In this tale most of the lines end with a pause; but note the over-running of the sense in ll. 344-60. The verse-paragraph is skilfully built, and Chaucer prefers to begin a paragraph with the second line of a couplet, so that the transition is less abrupt. The paragraphing of the Ellesmere MS. is shown in the text.

These brief notes do not profess to give an adequate account of Chaucer's metrical usage. They are intended to set a beginner in the way of reading for himself, and reaching his own interpretation of the rhythm through practice.

GLOSSARY

Not all the words in the text are given, nor all the references to the words included; but an attempt has been made to distinguish the many slight changes of meaning that have occurred since Chaucer's time; and students are recommended to test their interpretations by reading through the Glossary. The formation of English compounds is usually marked, but etymological notes are sparingly given, because they do not always help in the interpretation of the text. The following contractions are used:—OE. = Old English; OFr. = Old French; ON. = Old Norse; ME. = Middle English; N.E.D. = The Oxford English Dictionary; *sb.* = substantive; *pa.t.* = past tense; *pp.* = past participle; *imper.* = imperative; *impers.* = impersonal. *M.* before a line reference shows that it comes from *The Monk's Tale*; *n.* after a line reference shows that there is a note on the passage. The remarks on Spelling (p. 62) should be noted.

abhomynable, *adj.* unnatural, 287.

a-bove, *adv.* above, upwards, 187.

a-brayde, *pa. t.* woke with a start, 242.

a-byde, *v.* wait, 290, 314.

accord, *sb.* harmony, 113.

accordant (*to*), *adj.* in keeping (with), 70.

actes, *sb. pl.* histories, records, 370.

a-ferd, *pp. adj.* frightened, afraid, 153, 620, 655.

afferme, *v.* maintain the truth of, 359.

affrayed, *pp.* frightened, afraid, 512, 519. [OFr. *affrayer.*]

a-fright, *pp. adj.* afraid, 129.

after, *prep.* according to, 469; *adv.* afterwards, 360.

a-gaste, *v.* terrify, 322; *pp. adj.* agast, frightened, 123, 150.

a-gayn, *prep.* exposed to (sun), 503; towards (evening, &c.), 306, 312; *adv.* back: *turne agayn,* return, 448, 643.

a-go(n), *pp.* gone, past, 264, 440.

a-grief, *adv.* ill, unkindly (*lit.* in grief), 127 n.

agu, *sb.* ague, 194.

al, *adv.* quite, 211, 283, 383; *intensive,* 463. *See* al-so.

al-day, *adv.* constantly, 326 n.

als, *adv.* also, 20. *See* al-so.

al-so (. . . *as*), *conj.* as . . . as, 397, 445.

altercacioun, *sb.* wordy strife, 471.

al-wey, -way, *adv.* always, M. 773, 285.

an-hanged, *pp.* hanged, M. 765, 296, 374.

an-on, *adv.* forthwith, 43, 263, 511 [*lit.* 'in one'].

anoye, *v.* weary, displease, 23 n.

(a)poplexie, *sb.* apoplexy, an effusion—usually of blood—in the head, 75.

areest, *sb.* arrest, seizure, 134.

argument, *sb.* formal proof, 216.

a-right, *adv.* favourably, 130.

arrayed, *pp.* disposed, 271.

arwes, *sb. pl.* arrows, 164 n.

as, *conj.* as; see 102 n., 673 n., 177 n., M. 753 n.; *as it were,* like, 94, 413, 270 n. *See* al-so.

ascencioun, *sb.* ascension; rising above the horizon, 89; increasing altitude of the sun as the summer comes on, 190 n.

asure, *sb.* azure ; lapis lazuli, 96.

attame, *v.* open, begin on, 52. [OFr. *atamer* 'broach a new cask', &c.]

atte = *at the*, 247.

attempree, *adj.* moderate, 72.

auctorité, *sb.* authority, 209.

auctour, *sb.* author, authority, 218 n., 497.

avauntour, *sb.* braggart, 151.

aventure, *sb.* luck, 233 ; adventure, 420. [*ad-* became common in the sixteenth century.]

avoy! *exclam.* alas! 142.

a-vysioun, *sb.* vision, 348, 357, 386.

a-wait, *sb.* ambush, 459 n.

bad, *pa.t.* (of *bidde*) begged, 350.

bane, *sb.* slayer, death, 194.

bar, *pa.t. sg.* (of *bere*) bore ; carried, 613 n. ; behaved, 106. *See* beer.

batailled, *pp. adj.* embattled, crenellated, 94.

beer, *pa. t. sg.* (of *bere*) bore, 570. *See* bar. [OE. pa. t. pl. *bǣron.*]

bemes, *sb. pl.* beams (in a roof), 176.

bemes, *sb. pl.* trumpets, 632.

bene, *sb.* bean, worthless thing, 48.

benedicitee, *exclam.* bless us, 627 n. [Lat. imper. *benedicite.*]

berd, *sb.* beard, 154, 592.

bere, *sb.* bear, 169.

berk-yng, *sb.* barking, 620.

beryis, *sb. pl.* berries, 199.

beth, *imper. pl.* be, 564.

bi-fel, *pa.t.* (of *bifalle*) *impers.* it happened, 235, 425, 507.

bi-forn, *adv.* before, 377.

bi-gan, *pa.t.* began ; *with infin.*, M. 760 n.

bi-gyle, *v.* beguile, fool, 662.

bi-knewe, *pa.t.* (of *biknowe*), confessed, 295.

bi-tokne, *v.* betoken, M. 762.

bi-twixe, *prep.* between, 136, 552.

bi-wreye, *v.* reveal, 285.

blis-ful, *adj.* blessed, holy, 284 ; merry, happy, 431, 435.

bole, *sb.* bull, 169.

boon, *sb.* bone, 633 ; *blood and bones*, alliterative tag = all my body, 661.

bord, *sb.* table, 77.

boter-flye, *sb.* butterfly, 24, 508.

botme, *sb.* bottom, 335.

bour, *sb.* bower, bed-room, 66 n.

box, *sb.* boxwood, 632.

brak, *pa.t.* broke, 650. *See* breek. [OE. pa. t. sg. *bræc.*]

brasile, *sb.* a red dye from which Brazil takes its name, *Epilogue* (note to l. 43).

brast, *pa. t.* (ot *breste*) burst, 452.

braunes, *sb. pl.* brawn, muscles, *Epilogue* (note to l. 43).

breed, *sb.* bread, 78.

breek, *pa.t. sg.* broke, 622. *See* brak. [OE. pa. t. pl. *brǣcon.*]

breest, *sb.* chest, *Epil.* (n. to l. 43).

bren, *sb.* bran, 474 n.

brid, *sb.* bird, 115, 435.

brend, brent, *pp.* (of *brenne*) burnt, 599, M. 740 ; *pa.t.* brende, 602, 604.

brouke, *adj.* enjoy (use of), 534 n.

bulte, *v.* boult, sift, 474 n.

burned, *pp. adj.* burnished, 98.

but, *conj.* except, M. 773, 484 ; unless, 51.

butiller, *sb.* butler, 368.

by, *adv.* beside (her), 502.

byde, *v.* wait, 319. *See* abyde.

byle, *sb.* bill (of a bird), 95.

by-nethe, *adv.* beneath, downwards, 187.

cas, *sb.* (mis)chance, 438.

caste, *v.* cast, 427 ; *casten hem*, resolved, 309 n.

casuel-ly, *adv.* by accident, 335.

catel, *sb.* property, 61 n.

centaure, *sb.* centaury, 197 n.

certes, *adv.* verily, assuredly, 146.

certeyn, *adj.* (a)certain, 302, 469 ; *adv.* certainly, 551, M. 765.

chapitre, *sb.* chapter, 299.

cherl, *sb.* churl, rustic, 643.

choys, *sb.* choice, 480.

chuk, *sb.* cluck (of a cock), 408.

chukke, *v.* cry 'chuck', cluck, 416.

clappe, *v.* talk, prate, 15. [Metaphor from a bell.]

clepe, *v.* call, name, 104, 479.

clerk, *sb.* scholar, esp. one in holy orders, 469.

clokke, *sb.* clock, 88.

clomben, *pp.* climbed, 432.

cloos, *adj.* closed, shut, 566.

clos, *sb.* enclosure, yard, 594.

cold, *adj.* baneful, 490 n.

col-fox, *sb.* fox with black markings, 449. [lit 'coal-fox', found only here in English; but rare German *kohl-fuchs*, Dutch *koolvos*, and the description, prove the meaning. Examples of its use as a proper name in *Publ. Mod. Lang. Ass.* xxxix, 762 ff.]

colera, colere, *sb.* choler, the choleric humour, 162 n., 180.

coleryk, *adj.* choleric, having an excess of choleric humour, 189 n.

commune, *sb.* : *as in commune*, in common, commonly, 234.

compaignable, *adj.* friendly, 106.

compaignye, *sb.* company, 227.

compleyne, *v.* lament, 19, 583.

condicioneel, *adj.* conditional, 484. *See* note to ll. 477–84.

compleccioun, *sb.* mingling of humours, 158 n., 189 n.

congregacioun, *sb.* assembly, 222.

conseil, *sb.* advice, 487 ; secrets, 522 n.

conseille, *v.* counsel, advise, 179.

contek, *sb.* bloody quarrel, 166.

contrarie, *sb.* opposite, 514.

contree, *sb.* country, 302.

coomen, *pa.t. pl.* came, arrived, 221.

coral, *sb.* red coral (from Red Sea and Mediterranean), 93.

corn, *sb.* grain of corn, 409.

cote, *sb.* cottage, 70.

countrefete, *v.* imitate, equal, 555.

cours, *sb.* voyage, 333.

cride(n), *pa.t.* cried, 511, 605.

cronycle, *sb.* chronicle, 442. [OFr. *cronique* < Latin *chronica* < Gk. χρονικά 'annals'. The suffix *le* is due to confusion with *article*, &c.]

curteys, *adj.* courteous, 105.

damoysele, *sb.* damsel, mistress, 104.

dar, *pret. pres.* dare, 192 ; *pa.t.* dorste, 152.

daun, *sb.* master, 26 n., 205, 367, 546, 568.

dawen-ynge, *sb.* dawning, 116.

debonaire, *adj.* gracious, gentle, 105 [OFr. *de bonne aire*].

dede, *adj. wk.* dead, 272, 283.

deel, *sb.* part, bit ; *every deel* completely, 349 ; *never a deel* not at all, 390, 483.

deere, *adj.* dear, 123, 240, 339.

deigne, *v.* deign, *impers.* 415.

delit, *sb.* delight, 579 [OFr. *delit*, now modified by confusion with *light*, &c.]

delyver-ly, *adv.* deftly, smartly, 650.

departen, *v.* part (company), 227.

desport, *sb.* amusement, 25.

devyse, *v.* describe, 272.

deye, *sb.* dairy-keeper, 80.

deye, *v.* die, 140 ; *pa.t.* dyde, 30.

deyntee, *adj.* dainty, delicate, 69.

diffye, *v.* set at nought, 405 ; denounce, 390.

digestyves, *sb. pl.* medicines that help digestion, 195 n.

discrecioun, *sb.* sagacity, good judgement, 543, 552.

disese, *sb.* pain, 5.

disputisoun, *sb.* disputation, debate, 472.

dissymulour, *sb.* dissembler, 462.

divyne, *v.* suppose, 500 n.

do, *v.* do, cause, 664 n. ; cause (to

be), 254 n.; *han to do of* deal with, 485 ; *do no fors of* attach no weight to, 175.

doctour, *sb.* teacher, doctor; esp. one of the four great 'doctors' of the Western Church, viz. Ambrose, Augustine, Jerome, Gregory, 475.

doctrine, *sb.* instruction, edification, 676.

doghtren, *sb. pl.* daughters, 63 ; doghtres, 609.

doke, *sb.* duck, 624.

dong-carte, *sb.* dung-cart, 270.

donge, *sb.* dung, 252.

donge, *v.* to manure, 270.

dorste, *pa.t.* (of *dar*) durst, 152.

doute-lees, *adv.* without doubt, assuredly, 141, 342.

dradde, *pa.t.* (of *drede*), M. 738 n.

drecched, *pp.* distressed (by dreams), 121.

drede, *sb.* dread, 640.

drede(n) (*of*) *v.* dread, 163 ; *pa. t.* dradde, M. 738 n.

dreynt, *pp.* (of *drenche*), drowned, 316.

dwelle, *v.* tarry, 384.

dych, *sb.* ditch, 82.

dyde, *pa.t.* (of *d(e)ye*) died, 30.

dyghen, *v.* dye, *Epilogue* (n. to l. 43).

dystaf, *sb.* distaff : a cleft stick on which wool was wound in hand-spinning, 618.

ech, *adj.* each, 89.

eek, eke, *adv.* also, M. 750, 407.

eeris, *sb. pl.* ears, 137.

eet, *pa.t.* (of *ete*) ate, 67.

effect, *sb.* significance, consequences, 369.

ellebor, black hellebore, 197 n.

elles, *adv.* else, 27, 170.

endite, *v.* compose, express in writing, 441.

engendren (*of*), *v.* spring (from), 157.

engyne, *v.* rack, 294.

ensample, *sb.* example, 340.

entente, *sb.* purpose, 220, 657.

equynoxial, *sb.* celestial equator, 90 n.

er, *adv.* and *conj.* before, 196, 235.

erst, *adv.* previously, 515.

eschewe, *v.* avoid, evade, 572.

ese, *sb.* comfort, happiness, 6, 531.

espye, *v.* spy upon, 522.

estaat, *sb.* condition (of life), 9.

evere-mo, *adv.* for evermore, 49.

ever-ich-on, *pron.* every one, 53.

experience, *sb.* the test of practice ; actual observation, 212.

expowne, *v.* expound, 349.

ey, *sb.* egg, 79. [OE. *ǣg; egg* is ON.]

eyle, *v. impers.* ail, 124, 334.

fader, *gen. sg.* father's, 202 n.

faire, *adv.* well, elegantly, 106, 441.

falle, *v.* fall; happen, 366 ; *as it wolde falle* 'as chance appointed', 229. *See* fil.

faren, *pp.* (of *fare*), gone, 113.

faste, *adv.* (rapidly), volubly, 321 n.

fayn, *adj.* glad, delighted, M. 751 ; *adv.* gladly, 532.

feend, *sb.* fiend, 520, 623.

felawe, *sb.* friend, comrade, 219.

felonye, *sb.* crime, 274.

fer, *adj.* far, 302 ; *adv.*, 231 n.

fil, *pa.t. sg.* (of *falle*), befell, 310, 438.

flatour, *sb.* flatterer, 559.

flaugh, *pa.t.* (of *flye*), flew, 465. *See* 406 n.

flee, *v.* fly, 176 [OE. *flēon*].

fleigh, *pa.t. sg.* (of *flye*) flew, 573, 651. *See* fly.

flour, *sb.* flower, 97.

flowen, *pa.t. pl.* (of *flye*) flew, 625. *See* fly, flaugh.

fly, *pa.t.* flew, 406 n.

folye, *sb.* silly thing, 672.

foond, fond, *pa.t. sg.* (of *fynde*) found, 78, 258, 269 ; provided for, 63 ; *pl.* founde, discovered,

73

282; *pp.* y-founde, 416; founden, 212. [OE. pa. t. sg. *fánd*, pl.
fúndon.]

for, *prep.* for; because of, 31, 620;
against, 351 n; *with* to+*infin.*
M. 764 n., 13, 343, &c.; *conj.*
because, 548; since, 533; so that,
181; *for that* because M. 747, 606.

forn-cast, *pp.* foreseen, 451 n.

fors, *sb.* force; *ne do no fors of*
attach no importance to, 175.

for-slewthen, *v.* lose by sloth, 330.

forther-more, *adv.* moreover, 361.

for-wit-yng, *sb.* foreknowledge,
477. *See* forwoot.

for-woot, *pret. pres.* foreknows,
468, 482. *See* forwityng.

for-yete, *v.* forget, 188. [OE. *for-
gietan*; modern (*for*)*get* < ON.
geta.]

foul, *adj.* dirty, ill-groomed, ugly, 47.

free, *adj.* generous, 148, 503.

freend, *sb.* friend, 519.

fro, *prep.* from, 406. [OE. *fram*, *m*
dropped before following consonant.]

ful, *adv. intensive*: very, M. 767,
168, 189; *ful wo*, 172 n.

fume, *sb.* vapours, 157 n.

fumetere, *sb.* fumitory, 196 n. [Lat.
fumus terræ; the modern suffix
is due to confusion.]

fy, *exclam.* fie! 125, 142.

fyn, *adj.* fine, choice, 93.

gabbe, *v.* tell lies, 300.

gaitrys (beryis), *sb. pl.* buckthorn (?), 199 n. [OE. **gáte hrís*,
goat's bush, influenced by ON.
geit.]

galwes, *sb. pl.* gallows, M. 744.

game, *sb.* sport, fun, 25, 496.

gan, v. *with infin. forms a preterite*,
112, 237, 266, 307 n., &c.

gape, *v.* gasp in agony, *or* open the
mouth in death, M. 744; *pres. p.*
gapyng, 276 n.

gargat, *sb.* throat, 569. [OFr. *gar-
gate.*]

gentil, *adj.* gentle, high-born, 99.

gentillesse, *sb.* kindness, courtesy,
530.

gesse, *v.* guess, think, 4.

gilt, *sb.* guilt, 607.

glade, *v.* gladden, 45.

glad-ly, *adv.* eagerly, 458.

glad-som, *adj.* delightful, 12.

go(n), *v.* go; walk, 50 n.; (of
organs) play, 86.

governaunce, *sb.* control, 99; self-
control, 668.

grace, *sb.* (good) fortune, 393;
M. 743 n.

graunt mercy (of), *exclam.* (gra-
mercy), thank you (for). [OFr.
grant merci ' great thanks '.]

greet, *adj.* great, 206; gretteste,
superl., 218 n.

greve, *sb.* grove, 57 n.

greyn (*of Portyngale*), *sb.* a scarlet
dye from Portugal, *Epilogue*
(note to l. 43).

grote, *sb.* groat, fourpenny-bit,
192. [Dutch *groot.*]

grym, *adj.* fierce, 413.

ha! ha! cry to raise alarm, start a
chase, &c., 615.

habounde, *v.* abound, M. 758 [*h*
silent].

habundant, *adj.* abundant, 159 [*h*
silent].

han, *v.* have, 134; *pres. pl.* 2,
&c.

hap, *sb.* luck, M. 748.

happe, *v. impers.* happen, 221.

hardy, *adj.* brave, bold, 148, 273.

harrow, *exclam.* a cry for help, 279,
614. [OFr. *harou.*]

haven-syde, *sb.* shore of a haven,
305.

heed, *sb.* head, 75, 646.

heeld, *pa. t.* (of *holde*) held, 566.

heele, *sb.* health, healing, 184.

heere, *adv.* here, 297, 375.

heere(n), *v.* hear, 7, 21; *pa. t.* **herde,** 18.

heeris, *sb. pl.* hairs, 138. [OE. (Anglian) *hēr*; modern *hair* is from ON. *hár*.]

heet, *pa. t.* (of *hote*) was called, 83 n. *See* highte.

hegge, *sb.* fence, 452.

heigh, *adj.* high, exalted, M. 758, 680.

heighe, *adv.* high, 651.

heled, *pp.* (of *hele*), concealed, 289.

hem, *pron. pl. obj.* them, 165, &c.

hente, *v.* seize; *pa. t.* 569, 656; *pp.* 293, 592.

herbergage, *sb.* accommodation, lodging, 223.

herbe-yve, *sb.* herbive, *coronopus* (?) 200 n.

herkne, *v.* hark, 310 n., 444.

herte, *sb.* heart, 108; *of herte,* from the heart, 537; *herte deere,* beloved, 123.

herte-lees, *adj.* coward(ly), 142.

herte-ly, *adv.* with all (my) heart, 27.

hevene-kyng, *sb.* King of heaven, 30.

hevy-nesse, *sb.* sadness, 3, 21.

hewe, *sb.* hue, 257.

hewed, *pp. adj.* coloured, 103.

highte, *pa. t.* (of *hote*) is *or* was called, 65, 422. *See* heet.

hir(e), *pron. fem. poss.* her, 61, 502; *objective* **hire,** 71, 74; with impers. verbs, 68; see 12 n.; herself, 501; *pl. poss.* their, 163, 186, 530, 564, 606, 622.

hir-selven, *pron. reflex.* herself, 602.

hoo! *exclam.* stop! 1.

hoold, *sb.* keeping, 108 n.

hooly, *adj.* holy, pure, 353.

hoot, *adj.* hot, 191.

hostelrye, *sb.* inn, 228.

hostiler, *sb.* inn-keeper, 263.

hound, *sb.* dog, 134.

ho(u)s-bonde, *sb.* husband, 148, 606.

housbondrie, *sb.* economy, 62.

howpe, *v.* whoop, 634.

humour, bodily moisture, 159; cp. 162 n.

hyder, *adv.* hither, 44.

hydous, *adj.* hideous, 627.

hye, *adv.* high, 565. *See* heighe.

hym, *pron. obj. sg.* him; himself, 244, M. 738 n.; *dat.* with impersonal verbs, see 12 n. *See* hem, hir(e).

in, *sb.* inn, 260.

jade, *sb.* wretched nag, 46.

jangle, *v.* chatter, 669.

jape, *sb.* a trick, mock, illusion, 325.

jeet, *sb.* jet, 95.

jolif, *adj.* blithe, cheerful, 308. [Modern *jolly* has lost final *f.*]

kan, *pret. pres.* can, know how to, M. 745, 173; *pl.* konne, 155; *pa. t.* koude, 115.

katapuce, *sb.* catapuce, 199 n.

keen, *sb. pl.* cows, 65. [OE. *cū*, pl. *cŷ*; ME. pl. *kyn* (whence *kine*), but Kentish *keen.*]

keep, *sb.* heed, 244.

kepe, *v.* guard (himself), 350; watch over, 278.

konne, *pret. pres. pl.* can, 155.

koude, *pa. t.* (of *kan*) could, 115. [*l* in modern *could* is due to influence of *would.*]

kyn, *sb.* kin, lineage, 202.

kynde, *sb.* nature, instinct, 186, 430.

ladde, *pa. t.* (of *lede*) led, M. 740.

lak, *sb.* lack, shortage, 78,

large, *adj.* ample, 393; broad, *Epilogue* (note to l. 43).

lat, *imper.* (of *lete*), let, allow, 41, 391; *lat se,* 555 n. [*See* note to l. 74.]

latter, *adj. compar.* latter ; *latter ende*, end, 439.

lawriol, *sb.* spurge laurel, 196 n.

leere, *v.* learn, 340.

legende, *sb.* legend, 355 n.

lemes, *sb. pl.* flames, 164.

lene, *adj.* lean, 47.

lenger, *adv. compar.* longer, 268. [OE. *lengra*, mutated compar. of *long* adj.]

leoun, *sb.* lion, 413.

lese, *v.* lose, 376, 550; *pp.* lorn, 378.

leste, *v. impers.* it pleased, 307. See liste.

lette, *v. trans.* hinder, stop, 74 n.; postpone, 318 ; *intrans.* delay, 268, 323 n.

leve, *v.* leave, 419.

levere, *adj. compar.* rather, 354 n.

leye, *v.* lay (a wager), bet, 192.

lief, *sb.* lover, 113.

ligge(n), *v.* lie (in ambush, &c.), 459 ; lye, 239; *3rd sg. pres. indic.* lith, 276.

light-ly, *adv.* quickly, 173.

liste, *v. impers.* it pleased, 510; leste, 307. [OE. *lystan*; Kentish *lestan*.]

lite, *sb.* little (time), 347. [OE. *lȳt.*]

lith, *sb.* limb, 109 n.

logge, *sb.* (lodge), abode, 87.

logged, *pp.* lodged, 232.

logg-yng, *sb.* lodging, 229.

loken, *pp.* locked, held fast, 109 n.

lond, *sb.* land, 270; *in londe*, far away, 113 n.

loore, *sb.* teaching; wisdom, learning, 204, 430, 584.

lorn, *pp* lost. See lese.

losengeour, *sb.* false flatterer, 560.

lowde, *adv.* loudly, 15.

lust, *sb.* inclination, 40.

lyk, *adj.* like, 96, 98.

lyte, *adj.* little ; *gret and lyte*, ' of all kinds ', 166. See lite.

maad, *pp.* made, 134, 590.

maister, *sb.* master, 581.

maistow = *mayst thou*, 340.

malencolie, *sb.* melancholy (humour), 167, 180.

man, *sb.* and *indef. pron.* man ; one, 121 n.

maner, *sb.* kind (of), M. 771, 80 n.

mateere, *sb.* matter, subject, 472, 485.

maugree, *prep.* : *maugree youre heed* (*lit.* in despite of your head), in spite of all you can do, 646.

maze, *sb.* delusive thing, 327.

mervaille, *sb.* marvel, 310.

mery, *adj.* pleasant ; *ther mery is* where it is pleasant, 200 n. [OE. *myrige*, Kentish *merige*.]

meschaunce, *sb.* mischance, 575.

meschief, *sb.* trouble, 128.

messe-dayes, *sb. pl.* mass-days ; feast-days on which a layman must hear mass, 86.

mette, *pa. t.* (of *mete*) dreamt, M. 750 n., 236, 267, 317, 346, 373 ; *impers.* 128, 132, 312 ; *pp.* met, 160.

meynee, *sb.* following, 628.

ministre, *sb.* officer responsible for administration of law, 277, 292.

mooder, *sb.* mother, 530.

moost, *adv. superl.* for the most part, 77.

moot(e), *v.* may, 50, 210, 534; *pa. t.* moste, q. v.

moralité, *sb.* moral (lesson), 674.

mordre, *sb.* murder, 285 ff.

mordred, *pp.* murdered, 239, 275.

mordrour, *sb.* murderer, 460.

morwe, *sb.* morning, 259, 464, 488.

morwen-ynge, *sb.* morning, 536.

morwe-tyde, *sb.* morning, 250.

moste(n), *pa. t.* (of *moot*) had (to), 226, 540.

muchel. *adv.* much, 3.

multiplye, *v.* make (the world) populous, 579.

murie, *adj.* merry, 49 ; pleasant to

hear, musical, sweet-toned, 85 ;
compar. murier, 504.   See mery.

myrie, *adj.* merry, 51, 202 ; happy,
493 ; sweet, 525 ; pleasantly-
situated, 305.   *See* mery, murie.

myri-ly, *adv.* pleasantly, 506 ; with
enjoyment, 501.

na-mo, no more, 64 n.

na-moore, no more, 1, 663.

narwe, *adj* small, not roomy, 56.

nas = *ne was*, was not, 84, 245.

nat, *adv.* not, 24, 300.

na-the-less, *adv.* none the less, 205,
381.

ne, *negative particle* no, not, nor,
&c., 19, 25 ; negative doubled for
emphasis, 76, 574 ; combined
with verbs as *noot* = *ne woot, nys,
nas, nere.*

nede-ly, *adv.* necessarily, 478 f.

nedes, *adv.* necessarily, 468.

neer, *adv. compar.* nearer, 44.

nekke-bon, *sb.* neck(-bone), 296.

nere = *ne were, pa.t. subj.* were (it)
not (for), 28.

never(e), *adv.* never, 32 ; not (at
all), 17.

newe, *adv.* freshly, 283.

noght, *adv.* not, 481.

nones, *for the nones,* for the nonce,
for the occasion, 567. [ME. *for
than ones,* older *for than ane*
'for that one (time)', where *than*
is OE. *þæm,* dat. of def. art.]

nonne, *sb.* nun, 43 n.

noon, *pron. adj.* none, no, 35, 216.

noot, *pret. pres.* = *ne woot,* know
not, 17, 334, 494.

norice, *sb.* nurse, 349.

notabilitee, *sb.* thing worthy of
note, 443.

no-thyng, *adv.* not at all, 74, 510.

noyse, *sb.* noise, 627.

ny, *adv.* nigh, near, 384 ; *compar.*
neer, 44.

nyce, *adj.* foolish, 549.   [OFr. *nice*
< Lat. *nescius.*]

nygard, *sb.* niggard, miser, 149.

nyght, *sb. seven-nyght* (*old*) (sen-
night), week, 107.

nys = *ne ys* is not, 551.

o, oon, *pron. adj.* one, 224, 393 ;
218 n., 433.   *See* ones.

of, *prep.* of ; from, 386, 537 ; by,
382, 590; for, 204, 274 ; con-
cerning, 362 n., 563. *See* 84 n.,
163 n., 218 n., 553 n.

on, *prep.* on ; with *remembre,* 267.
See 470 n.

ones, *adv.* once, 568, 662. *See* nones.

oother, *pron. adj.* other ; *that
oother,* the second, 232 [hence
the tother].

orgon, *sb.* organ, 85 n.

orlogge, *sb.* clock, 88.   [OFr.
orloge < late Lat. *horologium.*]

out! *exclam.* (come) out! a cry for
help, &c., 614.

outre-ly, *adv.* utterly, 463.

out-sterte, *pa.t.* rushed out, 281.

paramours, *sb pl.* mistresses, 101.

pardee, *exclam* by God ! assuredly
18, 162.   [OFr. *par Dé.*]

parfit, *adj.* perfect, 470 n.   [OFr.
parfit, now remodelled after Lat.
perfectum.]

passe, *v.* surpass, 545 ; pass on,
173 ; *passe over,* pass on to something else, 496.

pasture, *sb.* act of feeding, 419.

pees, *sb.* peace, 669.

peyne, *sb.* pain, distress, 20, 588.

peyne, *v. refl.* take pains, exert
(one's self), 539.

pitous, *adj* arousing pity, 257.

plat, *adv.* flatly, bluntly, M. 767.

plesaunce, *sb.* pleasure, 100, 576.

pleye, *v.* amuse, be sportive, 40.

pleyne, *v.* lament, 587.

point, *sb.* detail, 256.

povre, *adj.* poor, 9.

powpe, *v.* toot (a horn), 633.

poynaunt, *adj.* (poignant), sharp-flavoured, 68.

preeve, *sb.* test of practice, 217 n.

present, *adj.* : *lif present*, present life, 215.

prive-ly, *adv.* secretly, 253.

propretee, *sb.* property, peculiar virtue, 186 n.

prow, *sb.* benefit, good, 184.

pryme, *sb.* nine a.m., 431. [Lat. *prima (hora)*.]

pyne, *v.* torture, 293.

quelle, *v.* kill, 624.

quod, 3 *sg. pret. pres.* quoth, 1, 251.

rad, *pp.* (of *rede*), read, 355, 546.

rage, *sb.* frenzy, 600.

real, *adj.* royal, regal, 410 n., 418.

recche, *v.* interpret, 130 n.

recche-lees, *adj.* disregardful, 341 ; thoughtless, 670.

reed, *adj.* red, 76.

regne, *sb.* kingdom, M. 774.

rekke, *v.* care, 48 ; *pa.t.* roghte, 574.

reme, *sb.* realm, 370. [OFr. *reaume*, *realme* ; the spelling with *l* gains ground after Chaucer's day.]

remenant, *sb.* (the) rest, 138.

renne, *v.* run, 417 ; *pa.t. pl.* ronne, 622 ; *pp.* y-ronne, 428.

rente, *sb.* revenue, 61 n.

repaire, *v.* go frequently (to), resort (to), 454.

repleccioun, *sb.* over-eating, 71 ; excess (of bodily humours), 157 n.

repleet, *sb.* full to excess, 191.

resonable, *adj.* equitable, 288.

rethor, *sb.* master of eloquence, 441. [Latin *rhetor*, Gk. ῥήτωρ.]

reulen, *v.* rule, govern, 278.

revel, *sb.* merriment, 437.

revers, *sb.* contrary, opposite, 211.

rewe, *v. impers.* : *it reweth me*, I am sorry for it, 331.

right, *adv.* just, 18, 167, 201, 299 ; *right anon*, immediately, 52, 292 ;

quite, 15 ; *right ynough*, quite enough, 2, 4.

roghte, *pa.t.* (of *rekke*) heeded, 574.

rome, *v.* walk leisurely, 132, 414. [Not connected with Rome—the vowel is open ǭ not close ọ̄.]

ronne, *pa.t. pl.* (of *renne*) ran, 622.

roore, *v.* utter a hoarse cry (of birds, &c.), 122.

sauf-ly, *adv.* safely, confidently, 442.

saugh, *pa.t.* (of *se*) saw, 133, 652.

say, *pa.t.* (of *se*), saw, 348.

sayn, *v.* say, 255. *See* seyn.

scole, *sb.* the schools, 471 n.

scorne, *v.* ridicule, 321 n.

se(e), *v.* see ; *pres. indic. pl.* **seen**, 360 ; *pa.t.* **saugh**, 133 ; **say**, 348 ; *pa.t. pl.* **syen**, 612 ; *pp.* **seyn**, 515. [OE. *sēon*, pa.t. sg. *seah*, pl. *sǣgon*.]

secree, *adj.* secret, discreet in talk, 149.

seinte, *adj.* holy ; *for seinte charitee*, 554. (But there is a St. Charity.)

seken, *v.* seek, search, 370.

sely, *adj.* simple, humble, 609.

sentence, *sb.* opinion, thought, 211 ; matter, 36 ; subject, 448 ; meaning, 399 ; 'noble sentiments', 584 n.

sette, *v.* : *sette nat a straw by*, set not the value of a straw on, 324.

sewe, *v.* pursue, 571.

seyn, *pp.* seen, 515. *See* se(e).

seyn, *v.* say, tell ; *with dat. pron.*, 315, 342, 593 ; *for to seyn*, M. 764 n. *See* sayn.

seynd, *adj. pp.* (of *senge* to singe), broiled on coals ? smoke-dried ? 79.

shadde, *pa.t.* (of *shede*), poured, M. 741.

shal, *pret. pres.* shall, must, 183 ; shall(be), 328 n. ; *pl.* shul, 184, 195 ; *pa.t.* sholde(n), 278, 376 n.

shal-tow = *shalt thou*, 252.

shente, *pa.t.* (of *shende*), injured, ruined, 75.

sherte, *sb.* shirt, 354.

shill(e), *adj.* shrill, 629.

sholde(n), *see* shal.

shoon, *pa.t.* shone, 95.

shot, *sb.* shooting; (a) missile (here an arrow), 583.

shrewe, *v.* curse, 660, 661.

shrighte, *pa.t.* (of *shriken*) shrieked, 596. *See* skrike.

shul, *pret. pres. pl.* (of *shal*) shall, 184, 193, 364. [OE. *sculon* pl.]

significacioun, *sb.* sign, foretokening, 213.

siker, *adj.* sure, 397; *compar.* siker-er, more trustworthy, 87. [OE. *sicor* < Lat. *securus*.]

siker-ly, *adv.* surely, 28, 505.

sith, *conj.* since, 329.

sklendre, *adj.* slender, scanty, 67.

skrike, *v.* shriek, 634 n.

slayn, slawe, *see* slee.

slee, *v.* slay; *pa.t.* slow, smote, M. 742; *pp.* slawe, 248; slayn, 256.

smal, *adj.* slim, narrow, 139, 542.

so, *adv.* (in adjurations), 22; *so have I!* so may I have . . . ! 300, 392; (forming an imperative), 679 n.

sodeyn, *adj.* sudden, 7.

sodeyn-ly, *adv.* suddenly, 438.

solas, *sb.* solace, delight, 8, 404, 437.

som-deel, *adv.* somewhat, 55.

som-what, *indef. pron.* something, 27, 39.

sondry, *adj.* (the) various, 370.

song, soong, *pa.t. sg.* sang, 504, 537.

sonne, *sb.* sun, 112.

soond, *sb.* sand, 501. [ME. vowels before *nd* were normally long.]

soong, *pa.t.* sang, 504. *See* song.

soore, *adv.* sorely, 294; with distress, *intensive*, 583.

sooth, *sb.* truth, 15, 255.

sooth-fast-nesse, *sb.* truth, 562.

sooth-ly, *adv.* truly, verily, 586.

sorwe, *sb.* sorrow, 487 n.

sorwe-ful, *adj.* sad, 438.

soverayn, -eyn, *adj.* supreme, 443, 581. [OFr. *soverein*, Late Lat. **superanus*.]

sovereyn-ly, *adv.* above all others, 596.

sper-hauke, *sb.* sparrow-hawk, *Epilogue* (note to l. 43).

sprynge, *v.* rise (of the sun), 112; grow (of flowers), 436.

stape, *adj. pp.* (of *steppe*) advanced, 55 n.

stente, *v.* cease, refrain (from), M. 745 n. *See* stynte. [OE. *styntan*, ME. *stinte*, Kentish *stente*.]

sterte, *pa.t.* start (up), 511; leap, 601. *See* stirte. [OE. *styrtan*, ME. *stirte*, Kentish *sterte*.]

stevene, *sb.* voice, 431, 525.

stikke, *sb.* stake, 82.

stille, *adj. lat . . . be stille*, leave alone, 677.

stirte, *v.* jump (up), 568; rush, 611. *See* sterte.

stonden, *v.* stand, 541.

stoor, *sb.* store; *telle no stoor of*, set no store by, 388.

strecche, *v.* stretch, 542.

streit, *adj.* scanty, short, 223; *streite swerd =* drawn sword (?), 591 n.

stremes, *sb.* streaming rays, M. 764.

streyne, *v.* constrain, 478.

stynte, *v.* cease, 391. *See* stente.

substance, *sb.* material, stuff, 37 n.

subtiltee, *sb.* cunning (trick), 553.

suffisaunce. *sb.* contentment, 73.

suffre, *v.* allow, permit, 580.

superfluytee, *sb.* excess, 161.

suspecioun, *sb.* suspicion; *fallen in s.* to be suspicious, 266.

sustres, *sb. pl.* sisters, 101, 502. [OE. *sweostor*, *swustor*; modern *sister* from ON. *systir*.]

swerd, *sb.* sword, 591.

sweven(e), *sb.* dream, M. 750, 155.

swich, *adj.* and *pron.* such (a), 12 n., 62 n., 111 n.

syen, *pa.t. pl.* (of *se*) saw, 612.

syn, *conj.* since, 107, 424; *syn that,* since, 577.

t' = *to* : *t'espye,* to spy out, 522.

taak, *imper.* (of *take*), take, 177 n.

tale, *sb.* tale; *tale tellen of,* take account of, 352.

talk-yng, *sb.* : *swich t.* such a discourse, 24.

tarie, *v.* tarry, wait, 304; delay, 181.

techen, *v.* direct, show the way (to), 183.

telle, *v.* reckon; *ne telle . . . no stoor of,* set no store by, 388; *pp.* toold, 352.

terciane, *adj. fevere terciane,* a fever increasing in violence every other day, 193 n.

thanne, *adv.* then, 92, 417.

that, *demonstr.* : *by that God above,* 143, 151.

that, *rel. pron.* who, which, that, 206, 301; see M. 741 f. n., 447 n.; *pron.* what, 2 ; *that that,* what, 20.

the, *def. art.* with names of materials: *the jeet,* jet, 95; *the fyn coral,* 93; *the burned gold,* 98; forming compound relative: *the whiche,* which, 186.

thee, *v.* thrive, prosper (in asseverations), 210 n., 666.

ther, *adv.* there: *conj.* where, M. 754, 239, 453; *ther as,* where, 236, 493.

ther-with-al, *adv.* besides, 327.

thilke = *the ilke,* that (same), 59, 90, 107.

this = *this is,* 291 n.

thise, *demonst. pron. pl.* these, 499; the, 34 n.

tho, *pron. pl.* those, M. 764, 185. [OE. *þā* pl. of def. art. *sē*.]

thogh, *conj.* though, 47.

thoughte *v. impers., pa.t.* (of *thynken*), it seemed, M. 753, 12 n.

thridde, *num. adj.* third, 247.

thritty, *num.* thirty, 424.

thurgh, *prep.* through, on account of, M. 748, 69.

thurgh-out, *prep.* through, 452.

thyng, *sb.* thing; *pl.* affairs, 323; *see* 12 n., 328 n.

thynketh (*me*), *v. impers.* it seems, 12 n. *See* thoughte.

tip-toon, *sb. pl.* tip-toes, 541.

to, *adv.* too, 159, 341.

to, *prep.* to ; for (= Lat. *ad*), 676 n.

to-morwe, *adv.* to-morrow morning, 315; *see* note to 250.

to-nyght, *adv.* this night, 160.

tool, *sb.* weapon, 150.

toon *or* **toos,** *sb. pl.* toes, 96, 565.

torment, *sb.* anguish, 600.

torne, turne, *v.* turn (over) 244; change to the opposite, 637; *t. agayn,* return, 448, 608, 643.

towaille, *sb.* towel, M. 755.

traisoun, traysoun, *sb.* treachery, 351, 557.

trespas, *sb.* wrong, 654.

trewe-ly, *adv.* truely, 356.

trone, *sb.* throne, M. 770. [OFr. *trone* ; modern *th* is due to classical spelling, Lat. *thronum.*]

tweye, tweyn, *num.* two, 79, 139. [OE. masc. *twēgen.*]

twies, *adv.* twice, 246.

tyde, *sb.* time, 330, 338 n.

under-stonde, *pp.* understood, learned, 114.

under-take, *v.* give one's word, 445.

undren, *sb.* time up to noon, 456.

un-to, *prep.* in addition to, 280.

un-war, *adj.* unexpected, M. 774.

up, *prep.* upon ; in asseverations : *up peril . . .* upon peril . . . 178 (cp. 'upon pain of death'. [OE. *uppan,* prep.; which in ME. coincides in form with the adverbs, OE. *up, uppe.*]

upon, *prep.* : *make shoutes upon,* raise hue and cry after, 631.

up-right, *adv.* face upwards, 276 n.

vanitee, *sb.* emptiness, illusion, 156; vain thing, 245, 325.

venym, *sb.* poison, 389 n.

verray, *adj.* very, actual, 217, 619; indeed, 125 n.

vers, *sb. pl.* verses, 547.

veyn, *sb.* : *in veyn*, in vain, to no purpose, 33.

viage, *sb.* voyage, 318.

vileynye, *sb.* bad turn, 521.

voys, *sb.* voice, 538.

waite, *v.* watch, 457 n.

war, *adj.* aware, 509; wary, M. 743.

ware, *v. imper.* beware (that), 190.

wax, *pa.t.* (of *wexe*) grewe, M. 756.

weel, wel, *adv.* well, 350, 389; *intensive* much, 561; with care, 361, 546.

wel, *sb.* : *wel was hym*, 110 n.

welkne, *sb. dat.* sky, M. 741.

wende, *v.* go, 315.

wende, *pa t.* (of *wene*) thought, M. 747.

werken, *v.* work; cause, 172 n.; *pp.* **wroght**, done, 482.

werre, *sb.* war, M. 746.

wessh, *pa.t.* washed, M. 754.

wexe, *v.* grow, become, 10. *See* wax.

wey-la-way, *exclam.* Alas! 614. [OE. *weg lā weg.*]

whan, *conj.* when, M. 775; *whan that*, when, 112; *see* M. 753 n.; *whan . . . thanne*, 91 f.

what, *interrog.* why, 280 n.; *what (that) indef. rel.* whatever, 468.

what-so, *pron.* whatsoever, 146.

wheer, *see* where.

wheither, *conj.* whether, 477. *See* wher.

whelp, *sb.* dog (not necessarily a puppy), 166.

wher, *conj.* whether, 365 n., 369, 518 n.

wher, *adv. interrog.* where, 518 n.

wher(e), *conj.* where; *wher(e) as* where, 6, 222; *see* n. to M. 753.

which, *rel.* which, who; *which that* who, 174; whom, M. 758, M. 768; *the whiche* pl. which, 186.

whilom, *adv.* formerly, once, 56, 219.

whitter, *adj. compar.* whiter, 97.

wight, *sb.* creature, person, 159.

wikke, *adj.* evil, 657. [The true form which *wicked* has replaced.]

wil-ful-ly, *adv.* deliberately, 330, 601, 666.

wise, *sb.* manner, 271.

with-oute(n), *prep.* without, 607; *adv.* on the outside, 82.

witnesse (on), *v.* take witness from, 470 n.

wit-yng, *sb.* knowledge, 483. *See* forwityng.

wlat-som, *adj.* revolting, 287.

wo, *sb.* misery, 172 n.

wode, *sb.* a wood, 570.

wol(e), *v.* will, intend, M. 773, 170; 2 *pers.* **wolt**, 329; *pa.t.* **wolde**, intended, 521. [The vowel in *wol, wolt*, is due to the rounding influence of the initial *w.*]

woldes-tow = *wouldes(t) thou*, 580.

wonder, *adv.* wondrously, 102; *adj.* strange, 312, 371.

wone, *v.* dwell, 450. *See* wont.

wont, *pp. adj.* (of *wone*) accustomed, 454.

wook, *pa.t.* (of *wake*) woke, 317.

woot, *pret. pres.* know(s), 37, 156, 389. *See* noot.

word, *sb.* speech, 406, 649.

world, *sb.* : *worldes blis*, happiness in this world, 434.

wort, *sb.* plant, vegetable, cabbage, 455 n., 508.

worthy, *adj.* 358, 582; that commands reverence, 477.

writ, *pa.t. sg.* (of *write*), wrote, 357. [OE. pa. t. sg. *wrāt*, pl. *writon.*]

wroght, *pp.* (of *werken*) done, 482.

wydwe, *sb.* widow, 55, 58.

wynke, *v.* close the eyes (*not* close

and open again rapidly), 540, 664.

wys, *adj.* sure(ly), 642.   *See* y-wis.

y-, prefix (OE. *ge-*) often used to form past participles, as :—

y-been, been, 531 ;

y-doon, done, 654 ;

y-founde, found, 416 ;

y-logged, lodged, 225 ;

y-ronne, run (*see* renne), 428 ;

y-seyled, sailed, 333 ;

y-warned, warned, 466 ;

y-write, written, 676.

yaf, *pa.t.* gave, 548.   *See* yeve.

ye, *exclam.* yea, yes, 14.

yeerd, *sb.* yard, enclosure, 81.

yet, *adv.* still, 571 ; yet again, 247 ; even now, 642.

yeve, *v.* give, 667 ; *pa.t.* yaf, 548. [OE. *giefan*; modern *give, gave* take initial hard *g* from ON. *gefa*.]

yis, *adv.* yes, 50.

y-wis, *adv.* certainly, assuredly, 2, 51, 433, 676. *See* wys. [OE. *gewis*, adj. 'certain'; from the ME. adverb arises the false archaism *I wis*, as if 'I know'.]

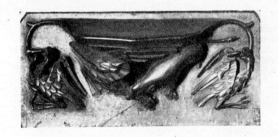

MIDDLE ENGLISH

SIR GAWAIN AND THE GREEN KNIGHT. Edited by J. R. R. TOLKIEN and E. V. GORDON. Crown 8vo. Pp. xxviii + 212. 7s. 6d. net.
At the Clarendon Press.

A STUDY OF GAWAIN AND THE GREEN KNIGHT, by G. L. KITTREDGE. 8vo. Pp. 332. 10s. 6d. net. *Harvard University Press.*

SELECT EARLY ENGLISH POEMS, edited by Sir I. GOLLANCZ. Fcap 4to.

I. *Patience,* an alliterative version of Jonah by the Poet of *Pearl.* Pp. 58. 5s. net.

II. *The Parlement of the Thre Ages.* An alliterative poem on the Nine Worthies and the Heroes of Romance. Pp. 116. 5s. net.

III. *A Good Short Debate between Winner and Waster.* An alliterative poem on Social and Economic Problems in England in the year 1352, with Modern English Rendering. 5s. net.

IV. *St. Erkenwald* (Bishop of London 675–693). An alliterative poem, written about 1386, narrating a miracle wrought by the Bishop in St. Paul's Cathedral. Pp. 112. 5s. net.

VII. *Cleanness.* An alliterative tripartite poem on the Deluge, the Destruction of Sodom, and the Death of Belshazzar, by the Poet of *Pearl.* Pp. 114. 5s. net.

VIII. *Pearl.* An English poem of the Fourteenth Century. Pp. 348. 25s. net.
Oxford University Press, London.

❡ Other Romances.

KING HORN, a Romance of the Thirteenth Century, with text of *Horne Childe,* edited by JOSEPH HALL. Pp. lvi + 238. 14s. net.
At the Clarendon Press.

THE LAY OF HAVELOK THE DANE. Second edition, revised by K. SISAM. Fcap 8vo. Pp. 212. 4s. 6d. net. *At the Clarendon Press.*

SIR EGLAMOUR, a Middle English Romance, edited by A. S. COOK. Pp. 148. 5s. net.
Yale University Press.

IWAIN, by A. C. L. BROWN; ARTHUR AND GORLAGON, by G. L. KITTREDGE. 8vo. Pp. vi + 276. 10s. 6d. net.
Harvard University Press.

STUDIES ON THE LIBEAUS DESCONUS, by W. H. SCHOFIELD. Pp. iv + 246. 8vo. 10s. 6d. net.
Harvard University Press.

MEDIAEVAL ROMANCE IN ENGLAND. A study of the Sources and Analogues on the Non-Cyclic Metrical Romances, by LAURA A. HIBBARD. Med. 8vo. Pp. viii + 342. 17s. 6d. net.
Oxford University Press, American Branch.

November 1929

¶ Piers Plowman.

THE VISION OF WILLIAM CON-CERNING PIERS THE PLOW-MAN, in three parallel texts, together with *Richard the Redeless*, by WILLIAM LANGLAND. Edited with preface, notes, and glossary by W. W. SKEAT. Two volumes. Pp. 636, xcvi + 484. 50s. net. *At the Clarendon Press.*

WILLIAM LANGLAND'S PIERS THE PLOUGHMAN (the B text, about A.D. 1377). Edited by W. W. SKEAT. Ninth edition. Fcap 8vo. Pp. xlviii + 216. 4s. 6d. net.
At the Clarendon Press.

PIERCE THE PLOUGHMAN'S CREDE (about A.D. 1394). Edited with introduction and notes by W.W. SKEAT. Fcap 8vo. Pp. xxxii + 74. 2s. 6d. net. *At the Clarendon Press.*

¶ John Gower.

THE COMPLETE WORKS OF JOHN GOWER, edited with intro-ductions, notes, glossaries, and fac-similes by G. C. MACAULAY. Four volumes 48s. net, or each volume 16s. net.

Vol. I. The French Works. Pp. lxxxviii + 564, with facsimile.

Vols. II & III. The English Works. Pp. clxxvi + 520, 656, with facsimile.

Vol. IV. The Latin Works. Pp. lxxviii + 430, with facsimile.
At the Clarendon Press.

GOWER'S CONFESSIO AMAN-TIS, selections edited with intro-duction, notes, glossary, and index, by G. C. MACAULAY. Fcap 8vo. Pp. lii + 252. 5s.
At the Clarendon Press.

¶ Chaucer.

THE WORKS OF GEOFFREY CHAUCER and Chaucerian and other Pieces, edited with introduc-tions and notes by W.W.SKEAT. Vols. I-VII, with portrait and facsimiles ; the set of seven volumes 105s. net, or each volume 16s. net.
At the Clarendon Press.

THE CLERKES TALE, illustrated edition, with introduction, notes, and glossary by K. SISAM. 1923. Pp. xxvi + 78. 2s. 3d.
At the Clarendon Press.

THE COMPLETE WORKS OF GEOFFREY CHAUCER IN POE-TRY AND PROSE, together with the two fragments of the *Romaunt of the Rose* not by Chaucer, with intro-duction, appendix of variations and emendations, and two glossarial in-dexes by the late WALTER W. SKEAT. 8vo. Pp. xxiv + 882. 6s. net.
At the Clarendon Press.

THE CANTERBURY TALES from the text of W. W. SKEAT, edition with glossary and brief notes on the language and metre (World's Clas-sics). 2s. net.
Oxford University Press, London.

THE NUN'S PRIEST'S TALE, illustrated edition, with introduction, notes, and glossary by K. SISAM. 1927. Pp. xlvi + 82. 1s. 6d.
At the Clarendon Press.

THE CHAUCER CANON, with a discussion of the works associated with the name of *Geoffrey Chaucer* by W. W. SKEAT. Crown 8vo. Pp. xii + 168. 3s. 6d. net.
At the Clarendon Press.

THE TALE OF GAMELYN. Second edition. Edited by W. W. SKEAT. Fcap 8vo. Pp. xl + 64. Paper boards. 1s. 9d.
At the Clarendon Press.

¶ Religious Works.

THE ORMULUM, edited by R. M. WHITE and R. HOLT. Two volumes. Fcap 8vo. Pp. lxxxviii + 598. 18s. net. *At the Clarendon Press.*

IACOB AND IOSEP, a Middle English Poem of the Thirteenth Century, edited with introduction, notes, and glossary by A. S. NAPIER. Crown 8vo. Pp. xxxii + 42. 3s. net. *At the Clarendon Press.*

THE PSALTER, or Psalms of David, and Certain Canticles, with a translation and exposition in English, by RICHARD ROLLE OF HAMPOLE, edited by H. R. BRAMLEY, with an introduction and glossary. 8vo. Pp. xxiv + 556. 21s. net. *At the Clarendon Press.*

THE MIRROUR OF THE BLESSED LYF OF JESU CHRIST, a translation from the Latin work entitled 'Meditationes Vitae Christi', attributed to Cardinal Bonaventura, made before the year 1410 by Nicholas Love, Prior of the Carthusian Monastery of Mount Grace. Edited with introductory note and glossary by L. F. POWELL. Crown 4to. Pp. 330. 21s. net. *At the Clarendon Press.*

THE EXEMPLUM IN THE EARLY RELIGIOUS AND DIDACTIC LITERATURE OF ENGLAND, by J. A. MOSHER. 8vo. Pp. xii + 150. 6s. 6d. net. *Columbia University Press.*

¶ Religious Lyrics.

RELIGIOUS LYRICS OF THE FOURTEENTH CENTURY. Edited by CARLETON BROWN. Crown 8vo, pp. xxiv + 358. 10s. 6d. net. *At the Clarendon Press.*

THE PENITENTIAL LYRIC IN MIDDLE ENGLISH. By F. A. PATTERSON. 8vo, pp. x + 207. 7s. 6d. net. *Columbia University Press.*

¶ Readers, &c.

SPECIMENS OF EARLY ENGLISH, edited with introduction, notes, and glossarial index. Three volumes. Fcap 8vo :—

Part I. From *Old English Homilies* to *King Horn* (A.D. 1150 to A.D. 1300), by R. MORRIS. Second edition revised. Pp. c + 554. 7s. 6d. net.

Part II. From *Robert of Gloucester* to *Gower* (A.D. 1298 to A.D. 1393), by R. MORRIS and W. W. SKEAT. Fourth edition. Pp. xl + 490. 7s. 6d. net.

Part III. From the *Ploughman's Crede* to the *Shepheardes Calender* (A.D. 1394-1579), by W. W. SKEAT. Sixth edition. Pp. xxxii + 550. 7s. 6d. net. *At the Clarendon Press.*

SELECTIONS FROM EARLY MIDDLE ENGLISH, 1130-1250, edited with introductions and notes by JOSEPH HALL. Crown 8vo, cloth, 21s. net. Separately: Part I, Texts, pp. viii + 222, 7s. 6d. net; Part II, Notes, pp. iv + 676, 15s. net. *At the Clarendon Press.*

FOURTEENTH CENTURY VERSE AND PROSE, edited with introduction and notes by KENNETH SISAM. Crown 8vo, pp. xlviii + 292. With a Glossary by J. R. R. TOLKIEN, pp. 168. 10s. 6d. net.

Separately, Text, Introduction and Notes, 7s. 6d. net. Glossary, 4s. 6d. net. *At the Clarendon Press.*

¶ Miracle Plays.

ENGLISH MIRACLE PLAYS, MORALITIES, AND INTERLUDES, being specimens of the pre-Elizabethan drama, by A. W. POLLARD. Seventh revised edition, 8s. 6d. net. *At the Clarendon Press.*

YORK PLAYS. The Plays performed by the Crafts or Mysteries of York on the day of Corpus Christi. Edited with introduction and glossary by L. TOULMIN SMITH. 3 plates. 8vo, pp. lxxviii + 558. 21s. net.
At the Clarendon Press.

THE ASSUMPTION OF THE VIRGIN, from the N-Town Cycle, edited by W. W. GREG. 8vo, pp. 76. Paper cover, 4s. 6d. net.
At the Clarendon Press.

¶ Miscellaneous Texts.

THE PROVERBS OF ALFRED, edited with introduction, notes, and glossarial index, by W. W. SKEAT. Fcap 8vo, pp. xlvi + 94. 3s.
At the Clarendon Press.

EARLY ENGLISH PROVERBS, chiefly of the thirteenth and fourteenth centuries, with illustrative quotations, collected and edited with notes by W. W. SKEAT. Fcap 8vo, pp. xxiv + 148, and portrait of John Wyclif. 5s. net.
At the Clarendon Press.

POEMS OF LAURENCE MINOT, edited with introduction and notes by JOSEPH HALL. Third edition, revised and reset. Fcap 8vo, pp. 176. 4s. 6d. net. *At the Clarendon Press.*

THE SERPENT OF DIVISION, by JOHN LYDGATE, the Monk of Bury, edited with introduction, notes, and glossary, by H. N. MacCracken, with three full-page reproductions from contemporary illuminations accompanying the text. 4to, pp. 76. 10s. net.
Yale University Press.

¶ Some Latin Texts.

OPERA HACTENUS INEDITA ROGERI BACONI, edited by ROBERT STEELE. 8vo, stiff paper covers. Fasc. I, 7s. 6d. net; II–IV, 10s. 6d. net each; V, 28s. net; VI, 25s. net; VII, 10s. 6d. net; VIII, 25s. net; IX, 22s. 6d. net.
At the Clarendon Press.

WALTER MAP'S DE NUGIS CURIALIUM, edited by M. R. JAMES. Anecdota Oxoniensia, Mediaeval Series, XIV. Crown 4to, rag-made paper, pp. 326. 18s. 6d. net.
At the Clarendon Press.

IOANNIS SARESBERIENSIS POLICRATICI Libri VIII recognovit commentario instruxit C. C. J. WEBB. Two volumes. 8vo, pp. l + 368 and viii + 510. 36s. net.
At the Clarendon Press.

NOVA LEGENDA ANGLIAE, as collected by John of Tynemouth, John Capgrave, and others, and first printed, with New Lives, by Wynkyn de Worde, 1516. Re-edited with fresh material from MS. and printed sources by C. HORSTMAN. Two volumes. 8vo, pp. lxviii + 506 + 732. 36s. net. *At the Clarendon Press.*

¶ Bibliography.

A MANUAL OF THE WRITINGS IN MIDDLE ENGLISH, 1050–1400, a source-book for the history of English Literature, by JOHN E. WELLS. Med. 8vo, pp. 956, with two Supplements: I (1919), pp. 90; II (1923), pp. 114; 23s. 6d. net. Supplements separately, each 6s. 6d. net. *Yale University Press.*